SECRET BLACK PROJECTS OF THE NEW WORLD ORDER

NEW WORLD
·ORDER·

Contents

Tim Swartz

Secret Black Projects of the New World Order

Abelard Productions Publishing

ISBN: 0-938294-80-6

Cover art by Wes Crum
Design by Chris Fleming
Editorial Direction by Timothy Green Beckley
Assisted by Carol Ann Rodriguez

©Copyright 1998 by Global Communications

For foreign or other rights contact:
GLOBAL COMMUNICATIONS
Box 753, New Brunswick, NJ 08903

Chapter 1

STEALTH TECHNOLOGY -- EARTHLY OR ET BASED?

SECRET BLACK PROJECTS OF THE NEW WORLD ORDER

Mysterious aircraft are secretly flying the skies above planet Earth. These strange craft are considered by some to be extraterrestrial spacecraft. Others are positive that the United States has developed and deployed highly top secret, antigravity ships disguised to resemble conventional aircraft. Perhaps the truth lies somewhere between.

Astounding leaps in science has yielded a new type of defensive weapon: Stealth Technology. Planes capable of dropping nuclear bombs can now fly invisibly into enemy airspace, drop a payload, and fly back out without being identified. Since the introduction of the Stealth aircraft to the general public, rumors have circulated that these jets might be using science so far ahead of current knowledge that it borders on the realm of science fiction.

UFO researchers have not dismissed speculation that these exotic aircraft are the result of acquired alien technology. However, the known science of Stealth is easily understood. The way most aircraft identification works is by constantly bombarding airspace with a RADAR signal. When a plane flies into its path, a signal bounces back to a sensor that determines size, and location of the plane. Other methods focus on measuring acoustic disturbances, visual contact, and infrared signatures.

●　●　●　●　●　●　●　●　●　●　●

STEALTH TECHNOLOGY

Stealth technology works by reducing or eliminating these attempts to identify aircraft. Panels on planes are angled so that radar is scattered and no signal bounces back to base. Planes are also covered in a layer of absorbent materials that reduce other signatures the plane might leave. Shape also has a lot to do with the "invisibility" of stealth planes. Extreme aerodynamics keep air turbulence to a minimum and cut down on flying noise.

The Stealth technology of today seems far removed from the technology of the World War II era. Is it possible that this technology could have been back engineered based upon the recovery of a crashed UFO outside of Roswell, New Mexico in the summer of 1947?

SECRET BLACK PROJECTS OF THE NEW WORLD ORDER

The B-2 Stealth Bomber has a "bat-wing" shape to reduce its RADAR cross-section, as well as visual recognition, especially on the horizon. Special low-noise engines are contained inside the body of the plane. Hot fumes are then capable of being mixed with cool air before leaving the plane. This fools heat sensors on the ground, and prevents heat seeking missiles from getting a lock on their targets.

Stealth technology was initially developed to bypass Soviet defense systems. However, the jets have proven their worth in other types of engagement. During the Gulf War, fifty-six Stealth Bombers flew 1,270 missions, and were never hit by enemy fire. The question remains though on how Stealth technology was developed? Problems that dogged research aircraft seemingly were solved quickly. This could mean that research involving exotic technologies, such as Stealth, could be far older then reported, Or that scientists could have received help from unexpected sources. Either way, the results are guarded deeply within the bowels of the Pentagon.

RELATION TO UFOS

The first reports of Stealth aircraft corresponded highly with reports of UFOs. Possibly the UFOs were in reality Stealth planes and other black budget aircraft. With the amount of secrecy surrounding Stealth materials, the truth may never be fully known.

Bob Oechsler, a robotics expert who claims he once was a NASA mission's specialist, said that the B-2 Stealth craft's primary propulsion system was removed from a recovered flying saucer. "The project utilizes an alien power plant, and it is disguised by the use of four GE-F118 engines with a modification called the GE-100. There's new technology today gleaned from recovered craft of nonhuman intelligence origin."

SECRET BLACK PROJECTS OF THE NEW WORLD ORDER

UFO investigator Pat Weissleader reported that he was on the trail of a photo from 1948, supposedly showing an axe-shaped UFO. "The man who obtained the photo works cleaning up contaminated soil at Norton AFB, near San Bernardino, California. He was looking over photo archives to see if there was evidence of toxic waste dumps on the base, then they would go to the spot and test it.

"The Air Force kept large photo boards of aerial shots of the base. He snuck out a photograph that seemed to show an unusual aircraft. I took the photo of the photo and put it into the computer, progressively enlarging it and printing it out. From the air it is a large triangle, slightly smaller on the back side. Blow ups make it seem that there are notches on the back side and perhaps some bumps on the front sides."

Norton AFB is one of the military facilities that was shut down in the military downsizing of the early 90's. Since it is close to San Bernardino, California, it has been suggested as a good place for a local airport. Federal guidelines mandate that before such a facility is turned over to civilian use, it has to be cleaned up from any pollution that has accumulated over the years of use.

It happens that Norton is particularly contaminated. Among other things, it is the site of the most radioactive well in the country. Not only are the usual clean ups needed, but people have been assigned to try and locate any sites of hidden pollution that might not be obvious in a visual examination.

One way this was done was to examine old photographs for evidence of oil spills or other contamination that may not be visible to an inspection today. When a potential site is located, ground samples are taken and tested to decide if any contamination exists. One of the team members was examining large photoboards in the archives and came across this picture.

Mysterious triangle-shape craft have been showing up in place of the formerly seen disc-shaped object. Triangles have been seen as far and wide as Phoenix and the British countryside. There are those who maintain they are made on Earth, while other researchers see them as manufactured by some other-worldly civilization.

SECRET BLACK PROJECTS OF THE NEW WORLD ORDER

MYSTERIOUS PICTURE

The picture is part of a larger photoboard and he took a picture of it with his camera. He used color film, although the original was black and white. Weissleader used Ez Photo software to enlarge the image of the triangular craft. He also manipulated the contrast and color to get a close up that enhanced the detail. The shadow of the craft is slightly wedge shaped, suggesting the nose was higher than the tail end. The close up view makes it appear as if the back edge was shaped something like the stealth bomber, with an almost zig zag form. There is also a suggestion of bulging curves on both sides. These shapes were consistent in a number of attempts to manipulate contrast, brightness and color to define the image.

NAZI SECRETS

Reports have surfaced over the years that Norton AFB may have been used as a testing area for a captured top-secret Nazi aircraft. The secret aircraft was alleged to have been a type of "flying wing" incorporating a completely new type of technology. Pat Weissleader may have come across the only known photo of this mysterious aircraft.

Could reports of UFOs actually be sightings of exotic, but purely terrestrial aircraft? These unknown aircraft could be using technologies that are so sophisticated that they are unrecognizable as earthly aircraft. Reports of sightings of mystery aircraft have coincided with reports of sightings of flying saucers. The state of Nevada has been the site of a major UFO flap for the past several years.

The question of whether an Unidentified Flying Object is reported as a sighting of a mystery aircraft or a flying saucer may have more to do with the predisposition of the individual observer than with the nature of the observed phenomena. The nature of many of the mystery aircraft reports are strikingly similar to other UFO reports. Strange lights seen moving erratically or at high speed in the sky have long been core elements of the UFO phenomena.

Investigations of flying saucer reports have consistently shown how even experienced and trained observers can misinterpret familiar phenomena seen under unfamiliar (or even familiar) circumstances. This precedent cannot exclude the existence of UFOs, although it does suggest caution in interpreting such reports.

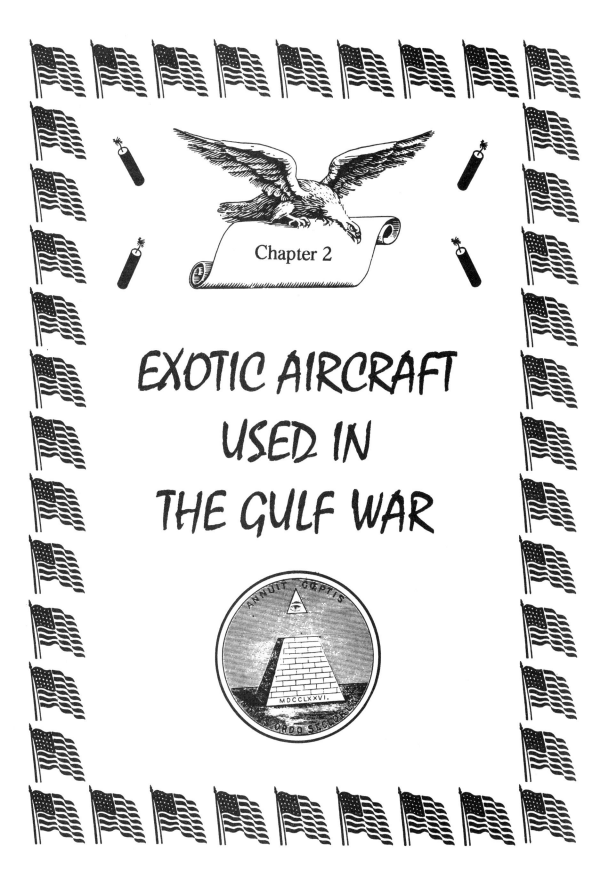

Chapter 2

EXOTIC AIRCRAFT
USED IN
THE GULF WAR

USAF/NORTHROP B-2

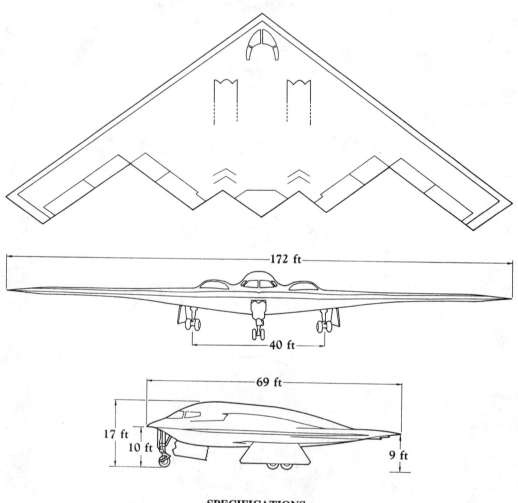

SPECIFICATIONS

• Crew:	2: Pilot & Mission Commander		• Gross Weight:	more than 350,000 lbs.
• Wingspan:	172 feet		• Payload:	more than 40,000 lbs.
• Length:	69 feet		• Unrefueled Range:	more than 6,000nm
• Height:	17 feet		• Range with one refueling:	10,000nm

SECRET BLACK PROJECTS OF THE NEW WORLD ORDER

The Stealth fighters and bomber are the most familiar of the new kinds of exotic aircraft. However, it wasn't until a few years ago that their existence was even acknowledged by the military. The Lockheed F-117A Stealth fighter was the worlds first operational combat aircraft designed to exploit the Stealth technology. With its unusual shape, the F-117A is now legendary due to its exploits over Baghdad in the Gulf war.

Development of the F-117A reportedly started in the early 70's when a number of US aerospace companies were experimenting with different technological designs to elude radar and surface to air missile defense Systems. In 1978 Lockheed's Advanced development Projects in Burbank, California nicknamed the "Skunk works" was contracted to turn an advanced demonstrator code named **HAVE BLUE**, into an operational, precision strike aircraft.

Using the expertise developed on the U-2 & SR-71 projects they were able to get the first F-117A airborne in about two and a half years. Tactical Air command received the first of its F-117A's in 1982 and its first combat unit, the 4450th Tactical Group achieved initial operational capability in October 1983 at Tonopah Test range in Nevada.

The F-117A employs a variety of technologies to mask it from detection by enemy radar. It is coated with a radar absorbent material (RAM) which absorbs the radar emissions. The faceted shape of the craft plays havoc with the reflection of the radar energy. Also, a special modified exhaust system reduces the amount of heat emitted by the turbofan engines. The internal design is also unique to the aircraft and remains classified. It is believed that the radar absorbent material is also used internally especially in the engine to reduce detection.

The name "Stealth Fighter" does not justify the use of this aircraft as it does not have the capability to fight air to air combat and has no defenses as chaff, flare, dispensers, and RADAR jamming. The F-117A relies completely on its Stealth capability and the night to avoid air defenses and enemy fighters. The armament on the Stealth is optimized for precision night attacks. It has forward and downward sighting infrared sensors for detecting and targeting guided munitions on selected targets. An internal navigation system enables the Stealth to find targets deep in enemy territory during night flight. The primary weapons are the Paveway series GBU-10 and GBU-27 laser guided bombs.

The F-117A was classified as a "black" program. Development and production was highly classified and done secretly over a number of years. However, in 1988 the USAF declassified the Stealth, the public and press were shown to some extent the Stealth's capabilities. Rumor has it that due to the strain on the pilots during night flights the Stealth was unveiled and the pilots were given free access to fly these aircraft in the daylight.

Actually, the real reason the Stealth aircraft were brought out into the open was that new, even more exotic aircraft were developed and ready for flight. Any reports of strange jets could be "explained away" as simply Stealth aircraft. During the Gulf war, the Stealth spearheaded the assault against Iraq hitting vital targets in Baghdad in the first few minutes and other vital air defenses were taken out to allow conventional aircraft to strike the interior of Iraq.

The F-117s attacked numerous targets in Iraq without even being fired upon or detected. Enemy targets included key communications centers, research, development, production and storage facilities for nuclear and chemical warfare. Numerous hardened aircraft shelters, bridges, railroad choke points, major highways and Iraqi defense system in Kuwait were also targeted.

The F-117A was the work horse of the Coalition strategic air campaign. The forty-two aircraft flew more than 1,200 combat sorties, over 6,900 combat

The government has attempted to explain away the existence of UFOs for half a century. This -- despite the fact -- that unexplainable phenomenon has been been picked up by radar operators and "flying saucers" have been observed and chased by our fastest aircraft. Are they ours or do they belong to some "foreign" technology?

hours and delivered more than 2,000 tons of explosives with pin point accuracy. In 1991 Lockheed proposed to extend the life of the Stealth by upgrading the existing aircraft to F-117A+ starting by replacing the engines. Other modifications included, improved Stealth capabilities, new all weather sensors, low probability of intercept communication, global navigation receivers, and an increase in the flight distance from the initial distance of about 570 nautical miles to 720 nautical miles.

The science of Stealth technology has been written about in many research papers and journals. However, as acknowledged by the Air Force, much of the technology used in the Stealth aircraft is still classified as Top Secret. The fact that much of Stealth is still shrouded in secrecy could be because certain aspects of Stealth and other exotic aircraft are using technologies that are unknown to most observers.

Paul A. LaViolette, Ph.D., believes that the Stealth aircraft are using what he calls Electrogravitic (antigravity) technology. LaViolette says that Electrogravitic technology was under development in the U.S. Air Force black research and development programs since late 1954. This research may now have been put to practical use in the B-2 Advanced Technology Bomber to provide an exotic auxiliary mode of propulsion. This inference is based on the disclosure that the B-2 charges both its wing leading edge and jet exhausts stream to a high voltage.

Positive ions emitted from its wing leading edge would produce a positively charged parabolic ion sheath ahead of the craft while negative ions injected into its exhaust stream would set up a trailing negative space charge with a potential difference in excess of 15 million volts. According to Electrogravitic research carried out by physicist T. Townsend Brown, such a differential space charge would set up an artificial gravity field that would induce a reactionless force on the aircraft in the direction of the positive pole. An Electrogravitic drive of this sort could allow the B-2 to function with over-unity propulsion efficiency when cruising at supersonic velocities.

SECRET BLACK PROJECTS OF THE NEW WORLD ORDER

B-2 BOMBER

For many years rumors circulated that the U.S. was secretly developing a highly advanced, radar-evading aircraft. Rumor turned to reality in November of 1988, when the Air Force unveiled the B-2 Advanced Technology Bomber. Although military spokesmen provided the news media with some information about the craft's outward design, and low radar and infrared profile, there was much they were silent about. However, several years later, some key secrets about the B-2 were leaked to the press.

Chapter 3

THE
MYSTERIOUS
DOCTOR BROWN

SECRET BLACK PROJECTS OF THE NEW WORLD ORDER

For nearly half a century there have been numerous individuals who claimed to have experienced face-to-face encounters with beings who they assumed were extraterrestrial. Such "contactees" like Howard Menger (author of From Outer Space To You) purported that such beings even landed on their property and posed along with their craft. Others who have studied these accounts first hand maintain that military intelligence or perhaps even the CIA played a part in "setting up" such encounters for there owe non-benevolent purposes.

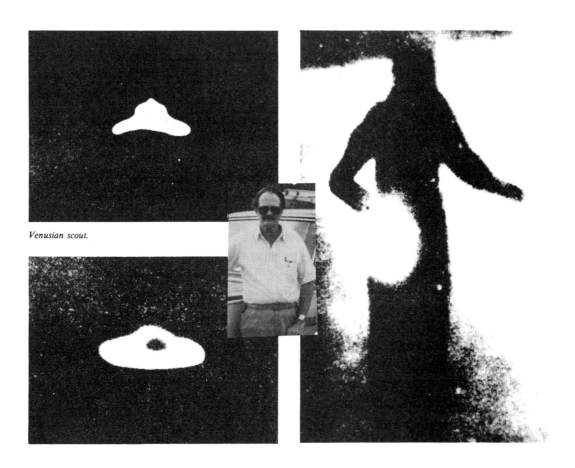

Venusian scout.

SECRET BLACK PROJECTS OF THE NEW WORLD ORDER

On March 9, 1992, *Aviation Week and Space Technology* magazine made a surprising disclosure that the B-2 electrostatically charges its exhaust stream and the leading edges of its wing-like body. Those familiar with the Electrogravitics research of American physicist T. Townsend Brown will quickly realize that this is tantamount to stating that the B-2 can function as an antigravity aircraft.

Beginning in the mid 1920's, T. Townsend Brown discovered that it is possible to create an artificial gravity field by charging an electrical capacitor to a high-voltage. He specially built a capacitor that used a heavy, high charge, accumulating (high K-factor) dielectric material between its plates and found that when charges with between 70,000 to 300,000 volts, it would move in the direction of its positive pole. When oriented with its positive side up, it would proceed to lose about 1 percent of its weight. He attributed this motion to an electrostatically induced gravity field acting between the capacitor's oppositely charged plates.

By 1958, he had succeeded in developing a 15-inch diameter model saucer that could lift over 110% of its weight. Brown's experiments had launched a new field of investigation that came to be known as Electrogravitics, the technology of controlling gravity through high-voltage electric charge.

Aviation Week obtained their information about the B-2 from a small group of renegade west coast scientists and engineers who were formerly associated with black research projects. In making these disclosures, these scientists broke a code of silence that rivals the Mafia's. They took the risk because they felt that it was important for economic reasons that efforts be made to declassify certain black technologies for commercial use.

Two of these individuals said that their civil rights had been blatantly abused (in the name of security) either to keep them quiet or to prevent them from leaving the tightly controlled black research and development community. Several months after

SECRET BLACK PROJECTS OF THE NEW WORLD ORDER

Aviation Week published the article, black world security personnel went into high gear. That sector of the black research and development community received strong warnings, and as a result, the group of scientists subsequently broke off contact with the magazine. Clearly, the overseers of black research and development programs were extremely concerned about the information leaks that had come out in that article.

Despite these concerns, information about the development of Stealth aircraft was earlier leaked during the Carter administration. In the summer of 1975, the first report claiming that a small Stealth fighter was being developed by the Air Force was published. Six months later, a second aviation journal said that "high priority was being given to the incorporation of stealth technology into fighter designs." The number of references to stealthy aircraft continued to grow over the following three years.

As the number of reports and speculation increased, President Carter's Secretary of Defense, Harold Brown, held a press conference to clear up the reports about Stealth aircraft. While he intended to provide a firebreak, Brown's confirmation of media speculation caused a maelstrom of Republican criticism. What was ignored, however, was that reports published years before gave much more detailed information than Brown's press conference.

Ignoring the fact that the F-117 had been officially recognized by the Carter Administration, President Reagan moved the program back into the black upon assuming office in 1981. Administration officials began referring to the aircraft as a "paper airplane," and "wishful thinking." While it was impossible to pull the wool over the eyes of aerospace junkies and journalists, this tactic did keep them guessing about the aircraft's precise design and capabilities.

SECRET BLACK PROJECTS OF THE NEW WORLD ORDER

Despite the uncertainties, throughout the early to mid 1980s, press reports, plastic model kits, and other speculation were accurate more often than they were not. Though the veil of secrecy was not completely opaque, it took sometime to correct several misconceptions concerning the program.

For example, the designation of the program remained somewhat obscure. Noting the numerical gap between the F/A-18 Hornet and the F-20 Tigershark, it was commonly assumed that the Stealth fighter's designation was F-19. Other reports suggested that the program was code-named Senior Prom. However, by 1987 these misconceptions had largely been resolved.

Based on first principles, it was assumed that the aircraft had rounded surfaces to reduce its radar cross section, such as were later incorporated in the more sophisticated B-2 and A-12 aircraft. Thus it came as something of a surprise when it was revealed that the F-117A had a faceted Shape. This misconception was derived from an overestimation of the state of the art in Stealth design in the 1970s.

Computational capabilities of that period were only able to analyze the radar signatures of relatively simple faceted aircraft designs. The use of more stealthy complex curved surfaces awaited the improved computers of the 1980s.

Despite these misconceptions, during the early 1980s an increasingly coherent picture of the Stealth fighter program emerged. At no point during this period was there any serious question in the public reporting as to the actual existence of the program. The credibility of the reports of the existence of the program was substantially increased by the crash of one of the aircraft in 1984, and another crash in 1986.

SECRET BLACK PROJECTS OF THE NEW WORLD ORDER

By the late 1980s the program entered a stage of development that involved public observation. As the aircraft began to take to the air they invariably drew public attention, despite the intense effort to keep them secret. Congressional inquiries into hundreds of missing contractor documents, films and photographs dealing with the aircraft were also difficult to cover-up.

Several rationales have been suggested for the Reagan Administration's re-unveiling the F-117A in 1988. One explanation is that the Reagan White House delayed the re-unveiling to wait for timing that would avoid the political overtones of Carter's election year announcement.

Another theory is that the re-unveiling was a damage limitation exercise, with officials deeming it better to officially inform the public of the F-117A rather than have the details wrung-out during an ugly court case involving Lockheed employees suing the government over alleged work-related injuries.

Perhaps the most compelling rationale for disclosure was that as the Air Force was thrusting the B-2 into the limelight to gain public and congressional support for that ailing project, there were fewer and fewer reasons to keep the F-117A in the dark.

The 1988 unveiling of the F-117A has not answered all the questions surrounding this program. How many F-117As were originally planned? A total of 59 were actually produced, with crashes having reduced the fleet to 56 aircraft. Press reports variously suggested that 72, 90, 100 or more aircraft were originally planned, though the number was reduced due to concerns over costs.

What mission was originally planned for this aircraft? With a program cost of nearly $150 million per aircraft (in 1992 dollars), the F-117A is often more expensive than comparable aircraft, such as the $20 million F-16, and can carry only a fraction of the bomb-load of its non-stealthy brethren.

The F- 117A gave a good account of itself during Desert Storm, this was more a function of its precision bombing capability than its stealthiness. The truth could be that the F-117A was built with acquired alien technologies for the purpose of defending the planet from otherworldly invaders. One of the best ways to defeat an enemy is to use their own weapons against them. The more conventional weapon systems were added to direct attention away from the aircrafts real purpose, to battle hostile extraterrestrials. Apart from technological inertia, the basis for the initial decision to procure the F-117A remains obscured by mountains of disinformation.

Chapter 4

BLACK PROJECTS:
THE AURORA...
DOES IT EXIST?

Lockheed 1985 Concept

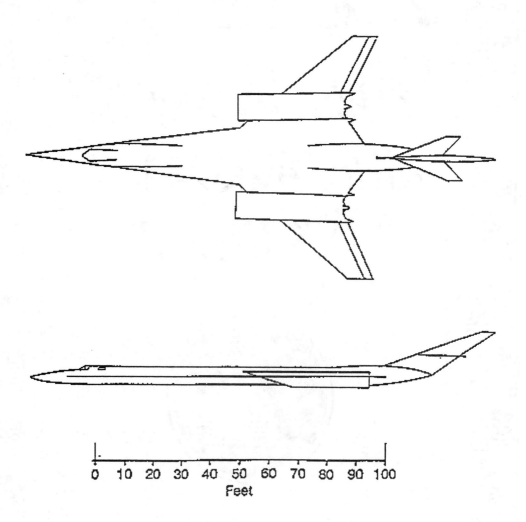

SECRET BLACK PROJECTS OF THE NEW WORLD ORDER

"Black Projects" are governmental projects considered technological secrets. These can range from laser and particle beam weapons, to top secret aircraft. The "Aurora Project" is the name given to one of these types of projects involving two new types of reported aircraft. These aircraft where observed in the south west US and are said to have been developed at highly classified government facilities in the Nevada desert.

According to reports, by mid-1992 Aurora was being flown from a base in the Nevada desert to an atoll in the Pacific, then on to Scotland to refuel before returning to the US at night. Specially modified tanker aircraft are being used to top up Aurora's tanks with liquid methane fuel in midair. The US Air Force was using the remote RAF airbase at Machrihanish Scotland, as a staging point.

Reports suggest that the mystery aircraft would "fly in at night before streaking back to America across the North Pole at more than six times the speed of sound. An F-111 fighter bomber is scrambled as the black-painted aircraft lands, flying in close formation to confuse prying civilian radars."

Probably the most compelling evidence for such flight tests are the series of unusual sonic booms above Southern California, beginning in mid to late 1991.
On at least five occasions, these sonic booms were recorded by at least 25 of the 220 US Geological Survey sensors across Southern California used to pinpoint earthquake epicenters. The incidents were recorded in June, October, November, and late January 1991.

Seismologists estimate that the aircraft were flying at speeds between Mach 3 and 4 and at altitudes of eight to ten miles. The aircraft's flight path was in a north, north-east direction, consistent with flight paths to secret test ranges in Nevada. Seismologists say that the sonic booms were characteristic of a vehicle smaller than the space shuttle. Furthermore, neither the shuttle nor NASA's single SR-71B were operating on the days the booms were registered.

One of the seismologists, Jim Mori, noted, "We can't tell anything about the vehicle. They seem stronger than other sonic booms that we record once in a while. They've all come on Thursday mornings about the same time, between six and seven in the morning." These "skyquakes" are a continuing phenomenon, with the most recent report over Orange County California, coming on July 20, 1996. It is reported that the "quakes" occurred around 3:00PM PST, fitting the "skyquake" pattern in the following respects:

- It occurred in a coastal area.

- Described as similar to an earthquake in some respects (rattling of loose objects, etc.) but also like a boom (but no distinct double bang as far as is known).

- Severe enough to light up government and media switchboards, but no known damage.

- Not an earthquake (CalTech sensors saw nothing).

- Local military bases deny any knowledge.

- No known other source (eg. explosion).

On April 5 and April 22, 1996 radio hobbyists in Southern California monitored transmissions between Edwards AFB's radar control facility (Joshua Control) and a high-altitude aircraft using the call sign "Gaspipe." The series of radio calls occurred at approximately 6:00AM local time on both dates.

Controllers were directing the unknown aircraft to a runway at Edwards, using advisories similar to those given space shuttle crews during a landing approach. The monitors recorded two advisories, both transmitted by Joshua Control to Gaspipe: "You're at 67,000, 81 miles out," and "Seventy mi. out, 36,000. Above glide slope."

Reported sightings of unusual high performance aircraft are not confined to the southwestern United States. More recently, such observations have also been reported in other parts of the United States, and in Europe. These reports are particularly intriguing because they are difficult to reconcile with an experimental test program, since there would be no reason for test flights to be conducted in Europe. These reports would indicate the deployment of a fully operational aircraft.

A mystery aircraft that some believe could be the Aurora was spotted by Chris Gibson, who for 13 years was a member of the ROC's aircraft recognition team. In this field, Gibson was considered to be an expert and produced an aircraft recognition manual for the ROC. In August 1989, while working as a drilling technologist on the jack-up rig "Galveston Key" located in the North Sea, a colleague pointed out to Gibson an unusual triangle-shaped aircraft overhead.

Gibson later recounted how this particular aircraft was like none he had ever seen. "I am trained in instant recognition, but this triangle had me stopped dead. My first thought was that it was another F-111, but there were no "gaps," it was too long and it didn't look like one. This might sound strange, but after doing aircraft recognition you get a feel for the shape of aircraft, what was called the "sit" in the past or what bird watchers refer to as "jizz." My next thought was that it was an F-117, as the highly swept planform of the F-117 had just been made public. Again the triangle was too long and had no gaps.

"After considering and rejecting a Mirage IV, I was totally out of ideas. Here was an aircraft, flying overhead, not too high and not particularly fast. A recognition gift and I was clueless. This was a new experience. My friend asked me what was going

Aurora

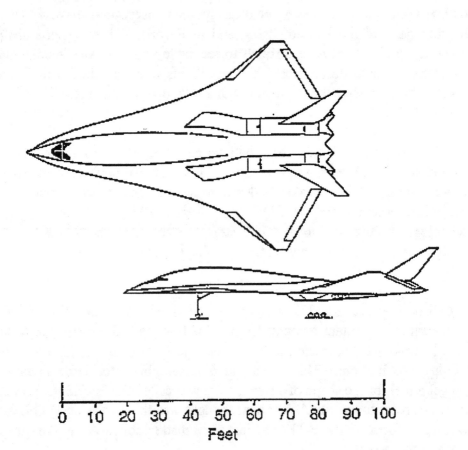

Drawn by Bill Sweetman, according to Chris Gibson this looks fairly close to what he saw over the North Sea off England.

on. I watched as the formation flew overhead and told him that the big one was a KC-135 Stratotanker, the two on the left were F-111 and that I didn't know what the fourth aircraft was.

"I watched the formation for a minute or two and went back inside. At the time I was writing the aircraft recognition manual and had a Danish Luftmelderkorpset "Flykendingsbog" in my briefcase. This is probably the best aircraft recognition book ever produced. I looked through it, but nothing matched. I then sketched what I had seen. I sent this sketch to Peter Edwards, who was a Group Officer in the ROC and was also on the recognition team. We discussed what to do about it but decided that if it was reported through official channels, it would be at best rubbished, at worst lead to trouble. Having signed the Official Secrets Act I didn't want to jeopardize my position in the recognition team. So I kept my mouth shut. I told other members of the recognition team in the hope that they could shed some light on the subject.

"On returning home I had a look through my book collection. The only aircraft which came close to matching what I had seen was a Handley Page HP115. It is obvious to me though, that what I saw was not one of them. Whether this aircraft was Aurora is debatable, my background precludes jumping to conclusions based on a single piece of evidence."

Aircraft spotter Steve Douglass has a theory of his own concerning the North Sea sighting. Douglass thinks that Gibson might have spotted the top secret A-17. The A-17 is reported to be a swing-wing aircraft, armed with bombs and self-defense missiles. In the lineup of stealth aircraft, the new bomber would carry an intermediate-size weapon payload, placing it between the Lockheed F-117A attack plane and the Northrop B-2 heavy bomber.

Swing wings add weight and complexity to an airplane, but they also provide unique benefits. Swung forward, the wings enhance lift and reduce fuel consumption. In this mode, range is improved, and takeoffs and landings can be made from relatively short runways. With its wings fully swept back, the aircraft assumes an aerodynamic drag-reducing delta shape suited for supersonic flight. In this shape, the A-17 would appear to ground observers to be triangle shaped.

Building Stealth into an airplane that can change the sweep angle of its wings poses a thorny technical challenge. As wing sweep changes, so do the directions in which the wing edges reflect radar beams. Designers can greatly simplify the radar-visibility problem, however, by concentrating on perfecting the airplane's shape with its wings fully swept. That's how the craft will look when it comes within range of hostile radars during an attack mission. The touchy part is minimizing radar reflections from the areas where the pivoting wings are joined.

The swing-wing plane is believed to have been developed by Northrop. The A-17 has major features in common with the YF-23, Northrop's losing bid to replace the Air Force's F-15 fighter. The A-17 shares the YF-23's underwing air inlets, the humps atop the aft fuselage that conceal its deeply submerged engines, and the long troughs used to cool exhaust by mixing it with fresh air. The bomber may have been secretly developed alongside the YF-23, or may have even preceded it and inspired elements of the fighter's design.

Grumman, the longtime builder of Navy aircraft, may also have had a hand in developing the A-17. The company has swing-wing experience gained from building its F-14 Tomcat Navy fighter. Northrop Grumman Corp., the company that is the result of a recent corporate merger, has new permanent offices at Cannon AFB, although the F-111s based there were built by General Dynamics.

The official explanation for Grumman's presence at Cannon AFB is avionics upgrade work on the EF-111 Ravens. The A-17's propulsion is likely furnished by a pair of high performance General Electric YF-120 turbofan engines developed for the advanced tactical fighter. These variable-cycle engines are efficient over a broad range of speeds and pushed the YF-23 past Mach 2 during flight testing. In a mode known as "supercruise" they also accelerated the YF-23 to Mach 1.6 without using fuel-gobbling afterburners. Therefore, the A-17 should be able to sprint to or from a target area at supersonic speed, if needed.

One unexplained set of observations was reported at Beale Air Force Base, the California facility that was long home to the SR-71. On two consecutive nights in late February 1992, observers reported sighting a triangular aircraft displaying a distinctive diamond-shaped lighting pattern, comprised of a red light near the nose, similar to the F-117 configuration, two "whitish" lights near what would be conventional wingtips and an amber light near the tail. While the wing lights are reportedly much brighter than normal navigation lamps, they do not illuminate the body of the aircraft. Observers claim the vehicle's wing lights are approximately twice as far apart as those on the F-117, and nose-to-tail light spacing is about 50 percent longer than that on the Stealth fighter, or on any other known aircraft.

SONIC BOOMS

Reports of "unusually loud, rumbling sonic booms" near Pensacola, Florida in November 1991 have also been associated with the Aurora program. At least 30 unexplained sonic booms have been reported in Southern California in late 1991 and early 1992. By mid-1992 noted aviation observer, Bill Sweetman, concluded that "The frequency of the sonic booms indicates that whatever is making them is now an operational aircraft." In early 1992 it was reported that, "RAF radars have acquired the hypersonic target traveling at speeds ranging from about Mach 6 to Mach 3 over a NATO-RAF base at Machrihanish, Scotland, near the tip of the Kintyre peninsula, last November and again this past January."

SECRET BLACK PROJECTS OF THE NEW WORLD ORDER

THE PULSER

There are two types of advanced aircraft being reported. One is nicknamed the "Pulser" aircraft. There have been many sightings of this aircraft by several different witnesses. When sighted, it has been described as "A high-speed aircraft characterized by a very loud, deep, rumbling engine noise (1-2 Hz pulse rate) reminiscent of heavy-lift rockets."

The smoke trail of the aircraft is described as segmented and in a linked sausage shape. It is also described as a high-altitude aircraft that crossed the sky at extremely high speeds. Both ground based and airborne observers have reported it to be seen flying at altitudes above 50,000 feet. Observers have reported seeing the aircraft as a single bright light that seldom changed direction. One observer estimated that it covered 350 miles in six minutes (3500 miles/hr).

These alleged secret aircraft may indeed exist. There has been research in to what are called Pulsed Detonation Engines (PED's) also called Pulsed Detonation Wave Engines. These are different type of engine than the pulse jet engines, which are already publicly know, and have been tested in aircraft. The PED's exhaust emission produces smoke trails that closely match eyewitness reports of the supposed Pulser aircraft. Simulations of theses engines are said to be able to propel large aircraft in the "Mach 0.2-3.0 flight regime."

PED's use shock waves created in a detonation to compress the fuel-oxidizer mixture before combustion. A cylinder chamber designed to support the detonation is constructed with a flat forward end that makes up the thrust wall. Air along with

LOCKHEED F-117A STEALTH FIGHTER

Max. gross weight: 52,500 lb.	Length: 65 ft. 11 in.	Crew: one
Speed: high subsonic	Span: 43 ft. 4 in.	Armament: internal weapons
Range: unlimited with air refueling	Height: 12 ft. 5 in.	USAF production: 59 aircraft

Developed for the U.S. Air Force by Lockheed Advanced Development Company, better known as the "Skunk Works," the F-117A Stealth Fighter is the first operational aircraft to exploit low observable stealth technology. Flown by pilots of the Tactical Air Command's 37th Tactical Fighter Wing, this single-seat fighter is designed to penetrate dense threat environments at night and attack high-value targets with pinpoint accuracy.

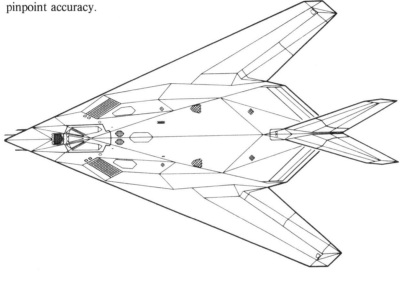

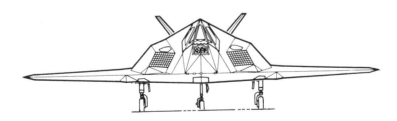

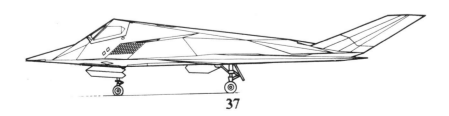

fuel is fed into the engine from behind the thrust-wall. The detonation wave created travels forward to the thrust wall at about Mach 4 and compresses the fuel-air mixture, promotes supersonic combustion and causes a pressure rise in the engine. The wave then strikes the thrust wall and rebounds accelerating the combustion products toward the nozzle. Some products are ejected by the wave to the outside air-stream through the air inlet openings creating a vortex outside the engine, then the cycle repeats.

There is very little information on the other reported aircraft. Eye-witness sightings describe a "triangular-shaped, quiet aircraft." This craft has been seen by many observers and flying with several F-117 Stealth aircraft. One unusual aspect is that the triangular-shaped aircraft has often been reported as flying at extremely low altitudes at a speed far slower then possible with conventional aircraft.

One witness reported that he could keep pace walking underneath a slowly moving large black triangle-shaped UFO. These UFOs generally move silently through the sky, and are often seen to be surrounded by a mysterious glow that could be associated with its propulsion system.

A report in *Aviation Week and Space Technology* in mid 1991 described a "triangular flying wing" reconnaissance aircraft, developed by Northrop (now Northrop Grumman) from 1982, designated TR-3A and nicknamed "Black Manta." According to the report, the aircraft had a length of about 13 meters, wingspan of about 19 meters, and a range of 5600 kilometers.

The aircraft had been deployed for trials to Alaska, Okinawa, Panama, and the United Kindom, and a few had been employed in Desert Storm in the reconnaissance role. The aircraft was apparently developed from a Northrop technology demonstrator known as THAP (Tactical High Altitude Penetrator), which first flew in 1981 and was similar in design, but slightly smaller. After this report however, nothing more was heard of the TR-3 for two years.

In 1993, Steve Douglass, videotaped a strange aircraft landing at White Sands Missile Range. Enhancement of the image revealed a formerly unknown aircraft, almost certainly the TR-3. Apart from having a curved trailing edge, it resembled a scaled-down B-2. It appears to be a single-seat, twin-engine, approximately triangular flying wing, which fits the description given in the earlier report.

Of the various "black" aircraft supposed to be flown by the USAF, more solid evidence exists for the TR-3 than any other top secret aircraft. Although it's difficult to judge the exact size of the aircraft from the Douglass videotape, the dimensions quoted in *Aviation Week and Space Technology* are plausible.

SUPER BLACK PROJECTS

Claimed sightings of unusual, high-speed, high-altitude, maneuvering vehicles during the last few years have led some to conclude that the United States has developed a fleet of new aircraft and is either testing them or already flying several types in operational service. It is suggested that because these programs are considered "super-super-black," military and other government officials routinely deny their existence.

While apparently the extent and nature of "black programs" are hidden from potential adversaries, and the public, what is less clear is the extent of knowledge and understanding that exists at the highest levels of the United States government. Are top decision makers fully aware of all that goes on in the bowels of government-financed aerospace design shops?

SECRET BLACK PROJECTS OF THE NEW WORLD ORDER

In recent years the Congress and senior government officials charged with oversight and funding of military programs have taken actions that seem patently inconsistent with the existence of these reported secret aircraft. However, it would not be unusual for only a very few political officials to be privy to these programs. Take for instance the secret development and deployment of the U-2 high-altitude reconnaissance aircraft. This vehicle was developed in response to Air Force requirements established in the fall of 1952. Lockheed was selected to develop the aircraft for the Central Intelligence Agency in November 1954, and the first prototype flew in August 1955 from Groom Lake Air Force Base in Nevada.

The first operational overflight of the Soviet Union was conducted on July 4, 1956. At the time there was no Soviet reaction to this first flight, the second mission shortly after produced a strong (though secret) protest from Moscow. Regular flights over Soviet airspace continued until a U-2 piloted by Francis Gary Powers was shot down on May 1, 1960.

"SKUNK WORKS"

The mystique of the Lockheed "Skunk Works" is based on a string of highly secret, exotic aircraft, notably the U-2 and SR-71. The genesis of the SR-71 program can be traced to 1954 when the US Air Force received an unsolicited proposal for a three-stage propeller-turbine powered aircraft fueled by liquid hydrogen and liquid oxygen. A contract was subsequently awarded to the Garrett Corp. to further explore technological possibilities of such an aircraft. Lockheed-California Company was a subcontractor on the project.

By 1957 the resulting research had metamorphosed into a CIA funded program, which began production in 1962. At various points in its existence this aircraft was termed the A-11, A-12, YF-12A, Senior Crown, Blackbird, Ox Cart, and Habu. To accommodate more sensors and crew, the program went through modifications that would eventually turn it into the SR-71. Because of it's impressive technological advances, and the CIA connection, the SR-71 was shrouded in secrecy. According to one report, even the Joint Chiefs of Staff were kept in the dark.

The aircraft's existence wasn't officially acknowledged by the Johnson administration until 1964, when it was unveiled to counter election year charges by Republicans that the Administration was not doing enough in the field of continental air defenses. Once it had been announced, however, the Johnson administration "became unusually secretive" about the A-11 (as the aircraft was mistakenly called) and refused to elaborate further on its mission or its capabilities. Top Air Force and Defense officials, including Secretary of Defense Robert McNamara, refused interviews. When pressed, McNamara referred to the aircraft as an "air defense interceptor."

Contemporary analysts considered this both a political effort to defuse a sensitive election campaign issue and an attempt to further obscure the SR-71's sensitive cold war reconnaissance mission. What had been largely ignored in this debate was that the possible existence of a high altitude, Mach 4 reconnaissance aircraft, had been reported as early as 1960.

The SR-71 wasn't a secret among those interested in the state of aerospace technology. The posited aircraft would incorporate a combination of a very slender fuselage and an "almost glass smooth skin" to improve lift/drag ratios. These early press speculations, the first official revelations of the existence of the program, and the wealth of information that subsequently emerged, did little to compromise the contributions of the SR-71 to the American intelligence community. For over a quarter of a century, the SR-71 remained an important reconnaissance asset, clearly proving the irrelevance of secrecy to the successful performance of this mission.

SECRET BLACK PROJECTS OF THE NEW WORLD ORDER

Popular Science magazine reported in January 1995 that then-secret F-117A Stealth fighters (developed and built at the Skunk Works) were ready to take part in the 1986 strike against Libya. The Stealth fighters were fueled, armed and waiting to depart from an air base in the Carolinas. However, an hour before they were scheduled to take off, Defense Secretary Casper Weinberger, fearful of revealing secret U.S. stealth technology if a plane were lost, cancelled the mission.

As a result, the attack was carried out, without the Stealth advantage, by a force of Air Force F-111, based in England and Navy F/A-18, A-7 and A-6 attack planes launched from aircraft carriers. One F-111 was downed by Libyan air defenses during the mission and its bombs hit civilian areas in Tripoli. The French Embassy was among the buildings damaged during the attack.

Because Stealth aircraft were not used in the raid, the element of surprise may have been lost. One day, such attacks may be carried out by a smaller more survivable force of radar-eluding attack planes derived from secret prototypes that are believed to be currently undergoing flight tests. Reports from aerospace observers indicates a black project aircraft that appears to be designed for precisely the kind of missions such as the Libya air attack.

Insiders who have seen it describe a fast, Stealth technology, swing-wing plane that looks like a cross between the current F-111 medium bomber and Northrop's YF-23 advanced tactical fighter prototype. High ranking officials are said to have gathered in secure hangers at two air bases to be given a covert peek at the new aircraft after its arrival under cover of darkness.

In 1994, the secret aircraft was observed circling high over Amarillo, Texas, for several minutes at midday. Chatter over a military UHF channel was intercepted when an aircraft with the unfamiliar call sign "Omega" was overheard reporting a hydraulic malfunction. The pilot said that he was dumping fuel in preparation for an emergency landing. The cloud of vaporizing fuel formed a wide, bright contrail, clearly pointing out the mysterious aircraft against the clear blue sky.

Binoculars revealed narrower contrails streaming from two smaller, darker-colored aircraft flying in formation with the Omega aircraft. These were F-111 chase planes, using the call sign "Duke" that were also dumping fuel to reduce weight before the early return to base. Unlike the conventional tails of the F-111s, the Omega airplane's tail was serrated with three aft-facing points. The stealthy plane appears to be the prototype of an attack aircraft that could replace the venerable F-111. This aircraft is known to fliers as the Aardvark, and has been in service in several versions since 1967.

SECRET SPACESHIPS

There is growing evidence that a mini-space shuttle, code named "Blue Eyes," was developed and made operational in 1992. Operating as part of the super-secret black budget projects, the new system is believed to be a space-plane which is about the size of an SR-71, and a large hypersonic mothership, which is said to resemble the experimental XB-70A strategic bomber built in the early 1960's.

Slightly larger than Concorde, the mothership may be used in a number of different roles, although it appears to have been specifically designed to carry the smaller space-plane on its back to a high launch altitude. Sightings of a large mothership sized aircraft began in 1990, when witnesses reported a new type of unidentified aircraft passing overhead. It was said to resemble a modernized version of the highly advanced, Mach 3 North American XB-70A Valkyrie bomber, that was developed for the USAF, but never put into production.

SECRET BLACK PROJECTS OF THE NEW WORLD ORDER

During the 1960's, two XB-70As were built and one was destroyed in a mid-air collision with a Lockheed F-104A Starfighter during a photographic mission. Soon after this disaster, the program was cancelled and the second aircraft was passed to NASA for high speed flight tests. The last Valkyrie eventually ended up in the Air Force Museum at Wright-Patterson AFB in 1969.

In 1991, reports began to appear of a new secret aircraft which resembled the Valkyrie. Although these reports were completely dismissed by aviation experts, more sightings were reported. In 1992, a reporter working for CNN saw an aircraft which resembled the XB-70A from a location near Atlanta, Georgia. Within a week of this sighting, a black colored XB-70A was observed in the vicinity of Lockheed's Helendale RADAR facility. This report coincided with a severe thunderstorm in the Groom Lake area, leading to speculation that the aircraft had been diverged from its original flight plan.

According to a story which appeared in the March 1994 issue of *Popular Science*, an arms control analyst claimed to have been shown a classified 1991 Landsat satellite image of Groom Lake. The photo revealed three large triangular shaped aircraft parked near the main runway. The analyst went on to say, "they are about the size of 747 airliners and remind me of the XB-70A bomber prototype from the 1960's."

It is possible that the 200ft long Super Valkyrie is simply a high performance, long range reconnaissance aircraft with a nuclear strike capability. Rumors that the Super Valkyrie is actually the Boeing B-3A cannot be substantiated. However, the suggestion that these aircraft were secretly developed with funding diverted from the Northrop B-2A program sounds quite realistic.

A high performance mothership remains the most likely role for the Super Valkyrie. A mini-shuttle or space-plane would ride on the back of the mothership.

Its high performance Pulse Detonation Wave Engines would lift the mini-shuttle high into the atmosphere, where the shuttle would detach itself from the mothership and then fly into low earth orbit. Videotape has been shot recently showing what appears to be a small, two man shuttle flying high over California, heading for either Edwards AFB, or the Groom Lake facility in Nevada.

THE THUNDERDART

On August 5, 1992, a Boeing 747 belonging to United Airlines encountered a UFO which may have been the secret space-plane. The airliner had just left Los Angeles International Airport bound for London. As it reached the vicinity of George AFB, California, the 747's Traffic Alert and Collision Avoidance System suddenly warned the flight crew that an aircraft was approaching at very high speed. There was no time for the 747 to take evasive maneuvers as the unidentified aircraft shot pass about 500-1000ft below the airliner. The pilot and co-pilot both described the UFO as having the forward fuselage of an SR-71, an overall lifting body shape and some kind of tail. The flight crew also reported the aircraft flew at hypersonic speed.

Testors Chief designer John Andrews, who made his name with the model of an F-19A Stealth fighter, quickly set to work on a model of the unknown aircraft. He dubbed the aircraft the *XR-7 Thunderdart*. When the models were released, *CBS Evening News* carried a story about the aircraft, with news anchor Dan Rather posing the question, "Does the United States military have a new top secret mystery plane?" The name XR-7 Thunderdart is purely fictional, although it has been recently reported that the space-plane is code named *Brilliant Buzzard*. The space-plane has almost certainly been based on NASA's X-24C proposals, or the highly classified USAF FDL-5 project.

The X-24C rocketplane was intended to follow NASA's Martin-Marietta X-24B lifting body test vehicle. Research had developed a one-man delta-shaped vehicle with a seventy five degree sweep. At the same time, the USAF was considering the black budget Lockheed FLD-5 as a successor to the X-15 rocket plane. If the FLD-5 was fully developed and tested, it would explain why the X-24C was cancelled by NASA, although the FLD-5 and the proposed X-24C may have been "black" and "white" versions of the same vehicle. The Thundardart is probably capable of reaching a low orbit, this will allow it to launch small military satellites, inspect those placed in orbit by other nations and destroy them if necessary. In addition, the space-plane could undertake global reconnaissance missions on short notice and possibly deliver space-to-ground kinetic energy or nuclear missiles.

The commissioning of the space-plane and its mothership could explain the Pentagon's decision to scrap the military space shuttle launch facilities at Vandenberg AFB. If Lockheed were chosen as the principal contractor for the space-plane and its mothership, this would explain the presence of a major black program which started in the mid 1980's and has shown up during subsequent analysis of the company's accounts.

Another factor which reinforced the belief that these projects were given the go-ahead in 1986, is the major re-development carried out at Groom Lake, which included a massive extension of the main runway. Groom Lake's improvements were initially attributed to the Aurora spyplane, but a large hanger was built, which would have been necessary for the Super-Valkyrie/space-plane project.

CODE NAMES AND DISINFORMATION

Debunkers of super-secret aircraft state that it is almost impossible to keep any such highly unusual planes secret for very long. However, as shown, there are any number of ways that such technologies can be kept secret for an extended period. The numbers of black budget projects reported in the media seem to suggest that rather than trying to protect a single program that actually exists, perhaps they have chosen to create a series of imaginary decoy programs, which would protect the real aircraft projects in much the way decoys protect ballistic missile warheads from interception by antimissile defenses. One method favored by the military and intelligence organizations is outright denial.

Time and again officials have lied about special weapon's systems and the technologies involved, only to later admit that such systems exist, and have been operational for a number of years. Another method is to disguise a black project with a series of different code names, each appearing to represent something different each time. Using disinformation has been used often to fool researchers, the press, and congress into complacency. William Scott, whose reports in *Aviation Week & Space Technology* have provided much of the information on mystery aircraft, concedes, "You have to be extremely cautious. There are a lot of guys who are good at misinformation."

The disinformation campaigns launched to persuade Saddam Hussein that the Marines would launch an amphibious assault on Kuwait, or to persuade Hitler that General Patton would launch the main Allied invasion against Callais are notable examples of this venerable gambit. The widespread reports that Area 51 in Nevada is home to captured extraterrestrial flying saucers, could be a disinformation ploy to disguise the secret black budget aircraft being tested there.

KOOK FACTOR

Any reports of unusual activity in the airspace above Area 51 are now generally ignored because of the "kook factor"associated with UFOs. However all disinformation in order to be effective must contain some elements of truth. The key is to try and figure out what is true and what is false. Unfortunately, the information is usually so garbled with useless material that it is impossible to weed out anything of value. What is known is that secret, black budget aircraft have been, and continue to be developed, using technologies that are so highly sophisticated the possibility exists that the science used could be the result of communications with unknown intelligence.

An extensive system of tunnels and underground bases are said to exist throughout the United States. Some of these tunnels and bases are occupied by aliens -- said to be cooperating with officials of the secret government or New World Order

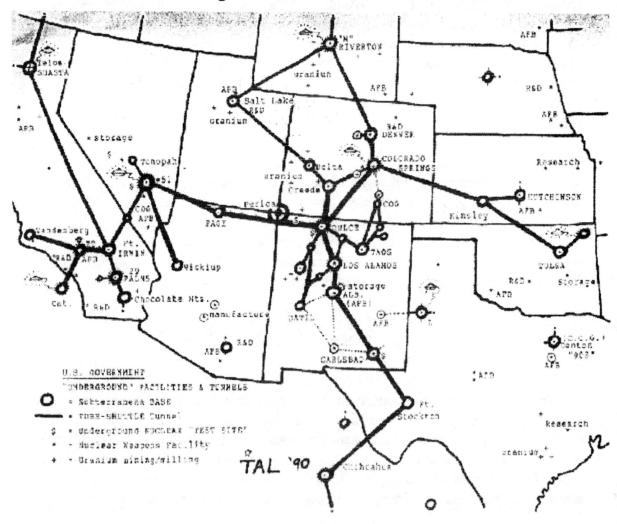

Chapter 5

UNDERGROUND
BASES OF THE
NEW WORLD ORDER

SECRET BLACK PROJECTS OF THE NEW WORLD ORDER

The late Phillip Schneider, in a series of lectures, claimed that due to his employment on several secret government projects, he was privy to information that "some would kill to keep quiet." In a speech given in 1995 at Post Falls, Idaho, Schneider detailed his involvement with black budget projects.

"I love the country I am living in, more than I love my life, but I would not be standing before you now, risking my life, if I did not believe it was so. The first part of this talk is going to concern deep underground military bases and the black budget. The black budget is a secretive budget that garners 25% of the gross national product of the United States. The black budget currently consumes $1.25 trillion per [2] years. At least this amount is used in black programs, like those concerned with deep underground military bases.

"Presently, there are 129 deep underground military bases in the United States. They have been building these 129 bases day and night, unceasingly, since the early 1940's. Some of them were built even earlier than that. These bases are basically large cities underground connected by high-speed magneto-leviton trains that have speeds up to Mach 2. Several books have been written about this activity. Al Bielek has my only copy of one of them. Richard Sauder, a Ph.D architect, has risked his life by talking about this. He worked with a number of government agencies on deep underground military bases. In around where you live, in Idaho, there are 11 of them.

"The average depth of these bases is over a mile, and they again are basically whole cities underground. They all are between 2.66 and 4.25 cubic miles in size. They have laser drilling machines that can drill a tunnel seven miles long in one day. The Black Projects sidestep the authority of Congress, which as we know is illegal. Right now, the New World Order is depending on these bases. If I had known at the time I was working on them that the NWO was involved, I would not have done it. I was lied to rather extensively. Basically, as far as technology is concerned, for every calendar year that transpires, military technology increases about 44.5 years.

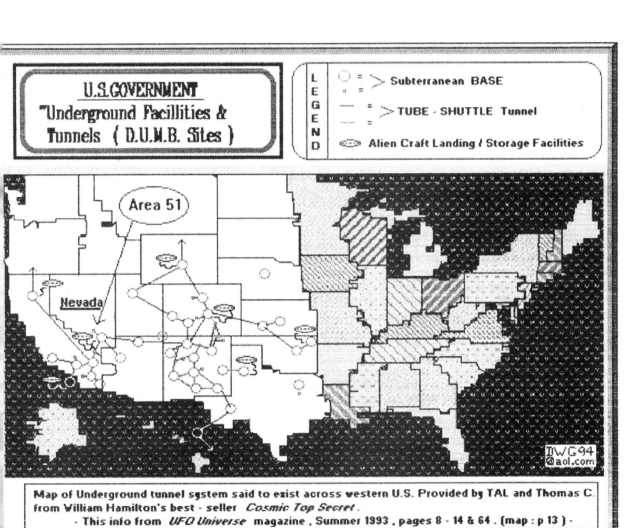

Map of Underground tunnel system said to exist across western U.S. Provided by TAL and Thomas C. from William Hamilton's best - seller *Cosmic Top Secret*.
- This info from *UFO Universe* magazine , Summer 1993 , pages 8 - 14 & 64 . (map : p 13) -

SECRET BLACK PROJECTS OF THE NEW WORLD ORDER

This is why it is easy to understand that back in 1943 they were able to create, through the use of vacuum tube technology, a ship that could literally disappear from one place and appear in another place.

"My father, Otto Oscar Schneider, fought on both sides of the war. He was originally a U-boat captain, and was captured and repatriated in the United States. He was involved with different kinds of concerns, such as the A-bomb, the H-bomb and the Philadelphia Experiment. He invented a high-speed camera that took pictures of the first atomic tests at Bikini Island on July 12, 1946. I have original photographs of that test, and the photos also show UFOs fleeing the bomb site at a high rate of speed. Bikini Island at the time was infested with them, especially under the water, and the natives had problems with their animals being mutilated. At that time, General McArthur felt that the next war would be with aliens from other worlds.

"Anyway, my father laid the groundwork with theoreticians about the Philadelphia experiment, as well as other experiments. What does that have to do with me? Nothing, other than the fact that he was my father. I don't agree with what he did on the other side, but I think he had a lot of guts in coming here. He was hated in Germany. There was a $1 million reward, payable in gold, to anyone who killed him. Obviously, they didn't succeed.

LEVEL SEVEN

"Back in 1954, under the Eisenhower administration, the 'federal' government decided to circumvent the Constitution of the United States and form a treaty with alien entities. It was called the 1954 Greada Treaty, which basically made the agreement that the aliens involved could take a few cows and test their implanting techniques on a few human beings, but that they had to give details about the people involved. Slowly, the aliens altered the bargain until they decided they wouldn't abide by it at all. Back in 1979, this was the reality, and the fire-fight at Dulce occurred quite by accident. I was involved in building an addition to the deep underground military base at Dulce, which is probably the deepest base. It goes down seven levels and over 2.5 miles deep.

"At that particular time, we had drilled four distinct holes in the desert, and we were going to link them together and blow out large sections at a time. My job was to go down the holes and check the rock samples, and recommend the explosive to deal with the particular rock. As I was headed down there, we found ourselves amidst a large cavern that was full of outer-space aliens, otherwise known as large Greys. I shot two of them. At that time, there were 30 people down there. About 40 more came down after this started, and all of them got killed. We had surprised a whole underground base of existing aliens. Later, we found out that they had been living in our planet for a long time. This could explain a lot of what is behind the theory of ancient astronauts. Anyway, I got shot in the chest with one of their weapons, which was a box on their body, that blew a hole in me and gave me a nasty dose of cobalt radiation. I have had cancer because of that.

"I didn't get really interested in UFO technology until I started work at Area 51, north of Las Vegas. After about two years recuperating after the 1979 incident, I went back to work for Morrison and Knudson, EG&G and other companies. At Area 51, they were testing all kinds of peculiar spacecraft. How many people here are familiar with Bob Lazar's story? He was a physicist working at Area 51 trying to decipher the propulsion factor in some of these craft.

"There are other problems. I have some interesting 1993 figures. There are 29 prototype Stealth aircraft presently. The budget from the U.S. Congress five-year plan for these is $245.6 million. You couldn't buy the spare parts for these black programs for that amount. So, we've been lied to. The black budget is roughly $1.3 trillion every two years. A trillion is a thousand billion. A trillion dollars weighs 11 tons.

SECRET BLACK PROJECTS OF THE NEW WORLD ORDER

"The U.S. Congress never sees the books involved with this clandestine pot of gold. Contractors of these programs: EG&G, Westinghouse, McDonnell Douglas, Morrison-Knudson, Wackenhut Security Systems, Boeing Aerospace, Lorimar Aerospace, Aerospacial in France, Mitsubishi Industries, Rider Trucks, Bechtel, plus a host of hundreds more. Is this what we are supposed to be living up to as freedom-loving people? I don't believe so.

"Still, 68% of the military budget is directly or indirectly affected by the black budget. Star Wars relies heavily upon stealth weaponry. By the way, none of the Stealth program would have been available if we had not taken apart crashed alien disks. None of it. Some of you might ask what the space shuttle is "shuttling." Large ingots of special metals that are milled in space and cannot be produced on the surface of the earth. They need the near vacuum of outer space to produce them. We are not even being told anything close to the truth.

"I believe our government officials have sold us down the drain, lock, stock and barrel. Up until several weeks ago, I was employed by the U.S. government with a Rhyolite-38 clearance factor, one of the highest in the world. I believe the Star War's program is there solely to act as a buffer to prevent alien attack, it has nothing to do with the "cold war," which was only a toy to garner money from all the people, for what? The whole lie was planned and executed for the last 75 years.

"Here's another piece of information for you folks. The Drug Enforcement Administration and the ATF rely on stealth tactical weaponry for as much as 40% of their operations budget. This in 1993, and the figures have gone up considerably since. The United Nations used American stealth aircraft for over 28% of its collective worldwide operations from 1990 to 1992, according to the Center for Strategic Studies and UN Report 3092.

SECRET BLACK PROJECTS OF THE NEW WORLD ORDER

"I don't perceive at this time that we have too much more than six months of life left in this country, at the present rate. We are the laughing stock of the world, because we are being hood-winked by so many evil people that are running this country. I think we can do better. I think the people over 45 are seriously worried about their future. I'm going to run some scary scenarios by you. The Contract With America. It contains the same terminology that Adolph Hitler used to subvert Germany in 1931. I believe we can do better. The Contract With America is a last ditch effort by our federal government to tear away the Constitution and the Bill of Rights.

Its quite apparent that we are not totally
in control of our own skies today!

Chapter 6

BLACK HELICOPTERS AND STRANGE FLYING TRIANGLES

SECRET BLACK PROJECTS OF THE NEW WORLD ORDER

Phil Schneider ended his speech with a warning about the secret black helicopters.

"There are over 64,000 black helicopters in the United States. For every hour that goes by, there is one being built. Is this the proper use of our money? What does the federal government need 64,000 tactical helicopters for, if they are not trying to enslave us. I doubt if the entire military needs 64,000 worldwide. I doubt if all the world needs that many.

"There are 157 F-117A stealth aircraft loaded with LIDAR and computer-enhanced imaging radar. They can see you walking from room to room when they fly over your house. They see objects in the house from the air with a variation limit of 1 inch to 30,000 miles. That's how accurate that is. Now, I worked in the federal government for a long time, and I know exactly how they handle their business."

Despite the seemingly wild claims of Schneider, something in his lectures must have caught the attentions of outside parties. Schneider soon began to fear for his life. He began telling friends that someone was out to "shut me up for good."

On January 17th 1996, Philip Schneider was found dead in his apartment in Willsonville, Oregon. While the county coroner declared Schneider died of natural causes, unusual circumstances surrounding his death soon became known. Schneider had in fact been strangled with a rubber hose wrapped around his neck three times and then knotted. The coroner revised her decision of death by natural causes, and instead said that Philip Schneider had committed suicide.

What makes the coroners new decision hard to believe was the fact that Philip Schneider had lost most of his fingers on his right hand in an accident years before. It was impossible for Schneider to tie the knot behind his head due to his disability.

SECRET BLACK PROJECTS OF THE NEW WORLD ORDER

Schneider's ex-wife, Cynthia Drayer, believes that Philip was murdered by special agents who were protecting government projects so secret that murder is simply another accepted way to hide the truth about black budget projects.

BLACK TRIANGLES

For a number of years reports of large, black, triangle shaped UFOs have intrigued investigators. The black triangles appear to superficially resemble Stealth type aircraft, the differences being that the black triangles are usually extremely large, fly at speeds slower then possible to maintain lift, and are totally soundless. Starting in 1983, the residents of the Hudson Valley area of New York and nearby Connecticut have seen some very strange objects in the night sky.

The UFOs have been described as larger than a football field with multicolored flashing lights. The object seems to take on a boomerang shape, but at times it also has appeared circular. Most witnesses report that it is a solid object made up of some type of very dark, gun-grey material. The object has been seen by at least five thousand witnesses that include police officers, scientists, and people from all walks of life. All say that the silent, slow moving UFO was something that they had never seen before and could not identify.

During 1989 and 1990, thousands of people in the nation of Belgium saw large triangular shaped UFOs in the sky. The sightings were often captured on film and video. The Belgian military sent jet fighters to chase some of the UFOs. In at least one instance, a military jet locked radar on one of the UFOs at the same time as it was being tracked by ground-based radar. Both radars measured the UFO doing maneuvers that would be considered impossible for a human aircraft, and because of the two separate radar readings, these findings are considered highly reliable. Finally a Belgian military spokesman went on TV to say that he could not explain what was happening.

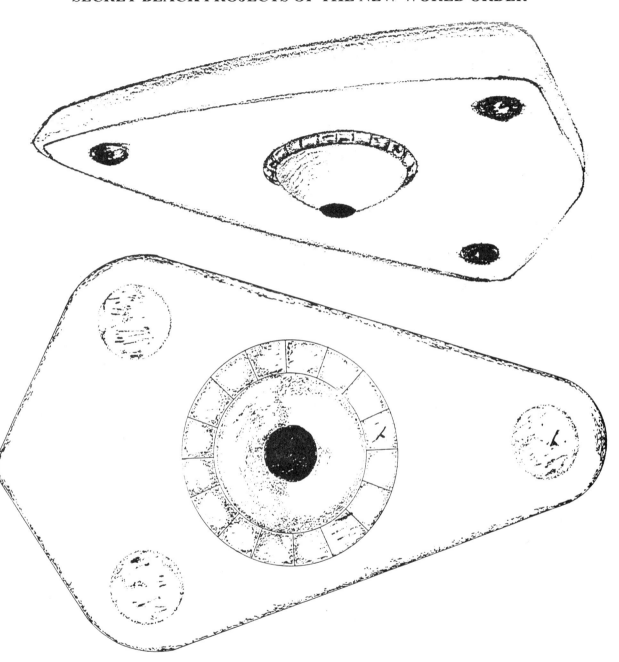

"Flying Platforms" such as this have been seen frequently over Belgium and other European nations -- without explanation!

Chapter 7

NEWLY REPORTED
UNEXPLAINED
BRITISH SIGHTINGS

SECRET BLACK PROJECTS OF THE NEW WORLD ORDER

Belgium is not the only country to report large triangle-shaped UFOs. Similar sightings have been reported in England. In March of 1993, a huge, silent, black triangle-shaped UFO flew over two air force bases in England. Military personnel immediately reported to the British Ministry of Defense, which then tried, but failed to explain what had been seen. Nick Pope, who headed the UFO investigation for the Ministry of Defense, later said he believed that this incident involved an aircraft of nonhuman origin.

A top BBC executive let slip recently that there is a D-Notice on media reporting of black triangles. The executive, who cannot be named, is the former producer of a very popular BBC science program. He told one investigator that the black triangle "craft," has been "heavily D-Noticed" by the government. Consequently the BBC will not be reporting on the enigmatic craft, no matter how many witness reports they receive.

According to the former science program producer, the reason the government has seen fit to slap a restrictive notice on reporting of the Triangle is because the government has secretly informed the BBC that the craft is part of a new secret military project, and as such must be protected under the secrecy laws. If this is the case, however, it surely begs the question: If the so-called Black Triangle is a secret military aircraft, then what is it doing hovering over residential areas and frightening people half to death? Something does not add up.

In an interview for a leading British UFO magazine, former British Ministry of Defense investigator Nick Pope reveals what his research has found.

"What was generally reported was a series of lights, flying in a perfect formation, with a third, much fainter light, our old friend the flying triangle. The lights were described as being in a triangle formation. It's difficult to say, of course, It's quite possible they could have been three separate things flying in formation, but the impression from talking to witnesses was that this was a triangular craft with lights mounted on the underside, at the edges.

"The most interesting reports, of course, were the ones that occurred at close distance. There was a family in Staffordshire that apparently saw this thing so low, and they described it as either triangular or diamond shaped, and they leapt into their car and tried to chase it. They did not succeed, although at one point they thought it was so low that it had actually come down in a field. It wasn't there when they got to it. They described a low, humming sound, a very low-frequency sound. They said you didn't just hear this sound, you felt it, like standing in front of a bass speaker.

"The really intriguing thing was that this object, whatever it was, then proceeded to fly over two military bases. It was seen by the guard patrol at RAF Cosford, about three or four people, who made an instant report of this, obviously because it had flown over their base. They checked radar, there was nothing on the screens, nothing at all, and there was nothing scheduled to fly. No military or civil aircraft should have been airborne in that area at all.

"They phoned the nearby base at RAF Shawbury, about 12 miles away from Cosford. The meteorological officer there took the call. He was a man with about eight year's experience of looking into the night sky and then doing the weather report for the next day. So he knew his way around objects and phenomena. Now, to his absolute amazement, he saw a light in the distance, coming closer and closer.

"That light eventually resolved itself into a solid structured craft that he saw again flying directly over the base, but at much closer proximity than the guard patrol at Cosford had seen it. He estimated that the height of the object was no more than 200 feet. Its size, he said, was midway between a C-130 Hercules transport aircraft and a Boeing 747. He heard the low hum, too. He had not spoken to any other witnesses, except the Cosford people, who had not reported the sound.

SECRET BLACK PROJECTS OF THE NEW WORLD ORDER

"Perhaps most disturbingly of all, he reported this thing throwing a beam of light down at the nearby countryside and fields just beyond the perimeter fence at the base. And this light was tracking backwards and forwards, he said to me, 'as if it was looking for something.' The beam of light then retracted, and the craft moved off. It was traveling very slowly, I should say, probably no more than 20 or 30 mph. Then it gained a little bit of height, and then it just shot off to the horizon in little more than a second. Needless to say, that was a description I had come across many times in other UFO reports, the virtual hover to the high-Mach accelerations in an instant."

MEANWHILE, IN AMERICA

Richard Dell'Aquila and Dale Wedge, investigated a series of triangle-shaped UFOs beginning around March 4, 1988 and seemingly centered on several Power Plants around Eastlake, Ohio. March 4, 1988 was a clear, crisp night. The stars were clearly visible, especially to the north over the lake where there are no city lights. Venus and Jupiter were bright and close to each other in the western sky.

At about 6:30 P.M., S.B. (name withheld) and her children were driving home to Eastlake along the lake shore when they observed a large blimp-like object with lights at each end, hovering over the lake and rocking up and down like a "teeter totter." One light was brighter than the other and was strobing. On arriving home, she asked her husband to accompany her to the beach for a closer view of the object that she described as "larger than a football field at arm's length."

She and her husband walked onto the beach. The noiseless object was gun metal gray and seemed to cause the ice on the lake to rumble and crack loudly in an unusual way that frightened her. The witnesses had to shout to be heard by each other, and were surprised that no dogs were out barking as would have been expected. After observing the object, the couple became concerned for the safety of their children in the car when the object revolved slowly about 90 degrees, coming almost overhead (about 1/4 mile high) and pointing it's "front" end down toward them.

They drove the children home (which was only one street up from the lake) and continued watching the object from their living room window that faces the lake. A neighbor was phoned and she and her son went to the beach, reporting the same thing. They took photographs which did not turn out (others from elsewhere would).

The object began to descend and the witnesses returned to the beach, where it was now observed to have red and blue blinking lights. It emitted five or six noiseless, intensely bright yellow triangular lights from its side. Mr. B. noticed a brighter light at the apex of the triangles. They intermittently hovered around the larger object, darted and zig-zagged into the night sky at velocities far in excess of known aircraft.

Mr. B stated the noiseless triangular objects were smaller than a one-seat Cessna, and traveled 50 mile stretches low over the ice in the "snap of a finger." They were said to be able to approach the shore, turn abrupt right angles due east toward a Power Plant about 12 miles away, climbing rapidly and returning, all within several seconds.

By this time, a Coast Guard patrol vehicle had arrived on the beach in response to S.B.'s several phone calls. The triangular objects came closer to the shore, causing the witnesses to become concerned that the lights on the Coast Guard vehicle would attract the objects and the lights were turned off. The triangles continued to fly off at high speed northward over the lake and eastward toward the Power Plant.

About an hour later, they returned one at a time into the large ship, which then landed on the ice. Several multi-colored lights now came on for about five minutes on the bottom of the object "in a wave like a movie theater sign." When these went off, the ice stopped making noise and everything became "dead silent." The object could no longer be seen within about a half hour and it was assumed to have gone below the surface.

The next day, huge pieces of broken ice were observed in the area of the landing. The Coast Guard informed Mr. and Mrs. B the following day that the Army and NASA had instructed them not to investigate the matter further or go out on the lake in their cutter to observe the ice in the area of the landing, since the matter was "out of their league and out of their hands." They informed the couple that all information was being forwarded to Wright Patterson Air Force Base and a facility in Detroit, Michigan. In response to a Coast Guard inquiry, Wright-Patterson refused to confirm or deny any interest in these activities.

Most black triangular shaped UFOs seem to have flight characteristics that indicate the use of unknown propulsion systems. Many black triangle aircraft are seen flying at speeds far slower then conventional aircraft can fly. Witnesses also notice that the aircraft can fly at extremely low altitudes with little, or no sound.

While traveling by car outside Biscay, Minnesota, Todd Madson and a friend sighted a pair of silent, triangle-shaped UFOs with some unusual flight characteristics. On Valentine's Day 1989, around 10PM, Todd Madson noticed a matching pair of red and green lights that were stationary in the sky, and at a very low altitude.

Todd's driving companion mentioned that she thought they were aircraft warning lights on "smokestacks," however Todd observed that there were no smokestacks in the area. The two pulled over and stopped, turning out the headlights to get a better view. Madson noticed that the objects were completely silent.

"My guess is that the planes were 400-500 feet off the ground when we first noticed them and they were just sitting there, probably 1/3 of a mile away towards the north, hovering above an empty farmer's field. There were two pairs of dull green and red stationary lights, with no strobes or other marker/running lights. So each object had one green light on one wing-tip and red on the other.

"Once we stopped, it appears that the hovering vehicles had 'noticed' that they had attracted some attention as they slowly started moving. At first they flew barely faster than walking speed, then picking up speed, they passed almost directly overhead towards the southeast.

"A sodium vapor (orange colored) streetlight provided a slight bit of illumination so the bottom of the craft could barely be glimpsed. The UFOs looked to be matte black(or possibly dark grey), no markings or lettering were visible nor was there any sort of visible lines for landing gear doors.

"The shape appeared triangular, with a possible extension to a tail of some sort towards the rear of the craft. Their shape was F-117-like, at least it is the closest match to any known aircraft that I am aware of. As they passed overhead there was a very quiet, muted, jet engine sound audible from the two craft, which was odd since they were at an altitude that should have made them much louder.

"The reason that they should have been louder for their height is that I had the distinct privilege of living under the main flight pattern for the Minneapolis-St.Paul International airport. I was used to seeing all sorts of commercial and military traffic at a height of about 1200 feet. Two jets at below 1000 feet would certainly be louder than this. I was left with the impression that I had witnessed aircraft that were using some kind of exotic propulsion system, maybe even antigravity. Due to their slow speed, I don't think they were the "black project" hypersonic/supersonic craft I've heard about. This was something that was powered by more then just jet engines."

Marc Whitford, Dinah Bertran, and Bruce Cornet witnessed and recorded a deliberate performance by a black triangle on May 17, 1997 near Montgomery, NY. During that performance the triangle flipped over and flew upside down and sideways for a distance before righting itself in a most unusual manner, which cannot be duplicated by a fixed-wing aircraft so low to the ground and at night. Then the craft did a series of turns without banking, descended very slowly, and disappeared below tree top level in an area where no airport or landing strip exists. As it did so it vented a plume of golden white plasma.

Marc was later told by someone, who claimed to work for Lockheed Skunk Works, that they had been given this performance by the U.S. military as part of their gradual release of information on a new top secret aircraft (possibly the triangular X-22A), which possesses technology allegedly derived from reverse engineered alien spacecraft. Whether this disclosure is true remains to be proven, because the area where the performance occurred has a history of UFO activity that goes back to the 1930's and possibly earlier.

In November 1993, in Seattle Washington, Gary Tenuta was driving close to the vast Boeing Aircraft Plant when he noticed three red lights low in the sky ahead of him. At first, Tenuta thought they must be the lights of a low flying plane, perhaps about to land. Then he thought they must be helicopters because a plane, even if it was landing, wouldn't be moving that slowly.

SECRET BLACK PROJECTS OF THE NEW WORLD ORDER

"I pulled my car off to the side of the road and rolled down the window to get a better look. I said to myself, "wait a minute, what the hell is that?" I opened the car door and stepped out, craning my neck to see the huge object directly over my head. It was a gigantic flying black triangle. There is no other way to describe it, a huge, black, flying triangle. I don't mean it was just sort of triangular shaped, like one of those wedge-winged jets or something. It was just one big three-sided, straight edged, triangle. It had a large red light on the bottom at each of its three corners. There was a high, gray cloud cover that evening, subtly lit by the Seattle city lights in the distance. Against this ceiling I could see the object like a huge, dense black silhouette."

The dark aircraft hung in the sky only about seventy-five to a hundred feet above one of the main Boeing hangars. It was slowly moving across the sky at a speed no faster then possibly five miles per hour. Tenuta felt it must be about the size of a football field. Suddenly he realized, as he stood there in the dark on this quiet empty street, the object didn't make a sound.

"Maybe more than anything else, that's what made the whole thing so eerie. Something that huge, that close, moving through the air at a snail's pace right over my head should be making some kind of a sound. A hum, a rumble, anything. It just moved across the sky like something out of a Steven Spielberg movie with the volume turned off.

"I looked up and down the street to see if anyone else was witnessing this silent event, but the street was dark and empty in both directions. I looked up again at the mysterious thing now blending into the dark horizon. I watched it until I couldn't see it anymore and then it was over. I got back into my car and pulled back out into the road. All the way home I just kept asking myself what I had really seen."

After Tenuta's strange encounter, a friend named Greg told Tenuta about his black triangle sighting while rock climbing with a buddy. One day, about 1981,

SECRET BLACK PROJECTS OF THE NEW WORLD ORDER

Greg was doing some hiking and rock climbing at a place called Lion Rock in Washington State. When he reached the plateau, he looked up and saw a dark triangle shaped object several thousand feet in the sky. As the two men stared in amazement, they noticed the object appeared to be getting larger. In a moment they realized it was in a free fall heading straight for them. They dove for the bushes and the object, which now could be quite clearly seen to be a craft, came to an abrupt stop about 150 feet above the ground and about 150 feet away from them.

Greg got out his field glasses to get a really good look at the surface of the craft. He noticed it really wasn't black but, rather, a very dark amber-hued brown. It had the appearance of being a molded piece. Greg estimated its size was about equal to a football field. He saw what seemed to be windows along one side and a glow of light coming from within the craft. Suddenly the craft let out an ear piercing screech and took off at an angle right over the two men. As it did so, the craft emitted a beam of white light which passed directly over them.

After the sighting, the two men suffered for about six months from what appeared to be a form of radiation sickness. Both men also experienced psychological repercussions for months after their strange encounter. Neither Greg or his friend has ever been back to Lion Rock for fear of seeing the strange aircraft again.

Black triangle UFO reports such as these may indicate that the United States military is flying aircraft that utilizes technology not normally known by most civilians. British writer Graham Birdsall reported on the claims of Tony Gonsalves, who says that the B-2 Stealth Bomber is a cover project for an even more secret aircraft.

Gonsalves thinks that the black triangle UFOs are the "real" top secret aircraft. "The black triangle aircraft uses a form of antigravity propulsion, that is why sightings of huge, slowly flying black triangles seem so unusual. The Stealth Bomber is a "cover" brought out to hide the fact that we now have antigravity propelled aircraft." Gonsalves claims that the B-2 is a "cut and paste job" and points out that so far, only four aircraft have been built. The four bombers combined have only recorded 600 flying hours. Gonsalves is convinced that another version of the B-2 exists. This secret aircraft is using some form of advanced technology which enables it to perform aerial maneuvers beyond our current understanding. These include the ability to hover, and move off at incredible speed.

Russian researcher Anton A. Anfalov says that two crafts of this type were allegedly seized by the Russians in 1945 in the mountainous areas of Eastern Europe occupied by the Red Army, and transported to Zhitkur. The drawing is not to scale, but the objects were known to be very large.

During the last few months there has been a dramatic increase in the number of reported sightings of mysterious flying triangles sighted over various parts of the United Kingdom. Some researchers are prone to blame their appearance on a tactical agreement with the U.S. for testing of anti-gravity devices.

Chapter 8

THE FORBIDDEN
TECHNOLOGY OF
NAZI SCIENCE

SECRET BLACK PROJECTS OF THE NEW WORLD ORDER

The mystery aircraft appear to use several different types of propulsion systems, including what appears to be a form of antigravity. Aircraft like the Stealth fighters and bombers could be the "conventional" types of jets put forward to the public to hide the fact that "nonconventional" aircraft are also up and operating. Reports of unusual aircraft are then simply dismissed as misinterpretations of conventional Stealth jets.

Retired Air Force Colonel Donald Ware has reported that, "the new Lockheed-Martin space shuttle (National Space Plane) and the B-2 (Stealth bomber) both have Electrogravitic systems on board," and that "this explains why our 21 Northrup B-2s cost about a billion dollars each." Thus, after taking off conventionally, the B-2 can switch to antigravity mode, and allegedly, fly around the world without refueling.

One researcher, after inspecting a Stealth F-117A fighter at Beale Air Force Base, reported that the F-117A also has hybrid propulsion and lift technologies. The aircraft utilizes conventional thrust for public takeoffs and landings, but switches to antigravity mode for extended cruising range, for lightning-fast maneuverability, and for shrouding the airframe in invisibility (by having its local counter-gravity field bend light around the airframe).

The notorious extremely unstable lift and forward-motion of the F-117A is merely temporary, until it moves into antigravity mode, where independent field propulsion provides stability. Unfortunately for the pilot who recently went down in an air show over Maryland, his Stealth fighter was in conventional jet-thrust mode at the time.

Colonel Ware is certain that the government eventually plans to release antigravity technology publicly. "Apparently this highly controlled military program was used to gain experience with 4th-density technology that may transform civil aviation after all national leaders choose peace."

Interest in antigravity as a form of propulsion has intrigued scientists and the military for decades. Many secret black research projects have been conducted over the years in the attempt to discover the secrets behind antigravity.

In 1967, Major Donald E. Keyhoe in an article called: *Saucers Secret: Antigravity*, written for *Flying Saucers* magazine, detailed some of the many antigravity projects being studied by the Air Force and private companies.

"Our government, hoping for a technical breakthrough, has set up forty-six different research projects on various aspects of gravity control. The Air Force is running thirty-three of these projects and the others are divided among five other agencies. Included in the forty-six government projects are experiments and research at two Air Force Laboratories (Flight Dynamics and General Physics Research), Radio Corporation of America, Massachusetts Institute of Technology and several technical engineering centers.

"In addition, official projects are being carried out at Barkley and Dexter Laboratories, Fitchburg, Massachusetts, Israel Institute of Technology, the Universities of California, Denver, Harvard, Indiana, Manchester (England), Maryland, Michigan, Minnesota, Ohio, Purdue, Stockholm (Sweden), Syracuse, Texas, and two New York schools - Queens College and Yeshiva Graduate School of Science.

"Of course, some government agencies have projects so secret that they are not publicly registered and cannot be revealed without permission. Private industry is also looking at the question of gravity control with new seriousness. A large number of giant corporations, including Bell Aerospace, General Electric, Hughes

SECRET BLACK PROJECTS OF THE NEW WORLD ORDER

Aircraft, Boeing, Douglas and many others, have set up gravity projects."

One leading scientist who was convinced that UFOs are spaceships using gravity control is the late Dr. Herman Oberth. Doctor Oberth, was a co-designer of the V-2 rocket, and later a U.S. special consultant at Huntsville, Alabama, one of the installations where antigravity research was conducted.

In 1961, Doctor Oberth stated that "With ordinary propulsion such violent accelerations and maneuvers seen with UFOs would endanger the ship. Also, the force would crush any creatures aboard against the rear or sides of the machine. However, with an artificial gravity field the force applies simultaneously to the passengers and the spaceship.

Even in swift changes of speed and direction, the ship is not strained and the passengers feel nothing. Energy, inertia and gravitational fields are only aspects of the same thing, and that it will prove impossible to separate them from each other. There are not yet known fields of force which can be used to accelerate material objects in a way similar to the force of gravity."

Under an Army contract, a University of Detroit team has built a 4,000-pound, specially wired rotor that spins at 100,000 rpm. With this unique device, scientists are testing gravitational radiation theories searching for a possible key to gravity control. Using gravity meters based on new principles of physics, Air Force teams make frequent flights around the equator and over the poles, to speed up world wide measurement of the Earth's gravitational pull. Tied in with this is a network of gravity stations and special projects all over the world.

Though no breakthrough has occurred (unless in highly secret projects), two significant facts have been established. 1. The Earth's G field is relatively weak, compared with the pull of gravity between planets and the sun. 2. There is a connection between gravity and electromagnetic fields. Some scientists still call gravity research a "lunatic fringe" notion. However, many now refuse to say that such a thing is completely impossible.

Major Keyhoe predicted in his 1967 article the military implications if we possessed attack aircraft that used antigravity propulsion. "Because of antigravity aircraft's tremendous speeds, the picture of possible military operations becomes hair-raising. Let's take as a basis the figure in a documented case at White Sands Proving Ground, where Navy scientists saw and tracked a UFO flying at 18,000 mph. Such terrific speeds could put bombers back into the picture in place of missiles. Attacks by antigravity bombers from base near major targets would take less than five minutes. If a "brush-fire" war broke out halfway around the world, a huge antigravity transport carrying a fully armed division or even an army could be on the scene in 40 minutes, or less."

Major Keyhoe's observation sounds very similar to today's black budget exotic aircraft.

GERMAN RESEARCH

For several years, Burkhard Heim, director of the German Research Institute of Field Physics at Goettingen, Germany, has been searching for the answer to the gravity riddle. Finally, Heim revealed that by direct experimentation he had discovered a positive lead to antigravity. The discovery involved an intermediate field, neither electromagnetic nor gravitational.

The results, Heim stated, if applied to space flight, would be direct levitation, conversion of electricity into kinetic energy without any waste, and "immunizing the occupants and the structures of such vehicles against any effects from acceleration of the vehicle, however great and violent."

After the first shock, several scientists examined Heim's claims. "His approach is not in conflict with known laws of nature, and it agrees with the quantum theory," A.R. Weyl said in an analysis for the British magazine, *Aeronautics*. "If Heim's theories are right, the amazing properties commonly ascribed to the `mysterious flying saucers' would be, in fact, sound physics and proper engineering."

Through Heim's work toward the goal of an actual antigravity force, researchers may discover new scientific laws and their work may invalidate old theories. Some scientists are already saying privately that Einstein's famous "general theory of relativity" may turn out to be totally fallacious. Newton's law has also come under attack. However, Robert Forward, Gravity expert of Hughes Aircraft Company, uses the Einstein theory to show that it is possible to partially nullify the Earth's gravitational field.

The amount of nullification obtainable with present-day technology is extremely small, however. Forward predicts that some day, when our technology is greatly advanced, we will be able to "create artificial gravity fields at will." If the exotic aircraft flying the planets skies are any indication, then antigravity has already been successfully developed and deployed.

Scientists in Finland have recently stated that they may have discovered the technology used by secret black budget aircraft. Measuring about 12" across, the device is said to reduce significantly the weight of anything suspended over it. The claim, which has been rigorously examined by scientists, could spark a technological revolution, unless the military tries to put a top secret clamp on the research.

By combating gravity, the most ubiquitous force in the universe, everything from transport to power generation could be transformed. *The Sunday Telegraph* has learned that NASA is taking the claims seriously, and is funding research into how the antigravity effect could be turned into a means of flight.

The researchers at the Tampere University of Technology in Finland, who discovered the effect, say it could form the heart of a new power source, in which it is used to drive fluids' past electricity-generating turbines. According to Dr Eugene Podkletnov, who led the research, the discovery was accidental. It emerged during routine work on so-called "superconductivity," the ability of some materials to lose their electrical resistance at very low temperatures.

The team was carrying out tests on a rapidly spinning disc of superconducting ceramic suspended in the magnetic field of three electric coils, all enclosed in a low-temperature vessel called a cryostat. "One of my friends came in and he was smoking his pipe," Dr Podkletnov said. "He put some smoke over the cryostat and we saw that the smoke was going to the ceiling all the time. It was amazing, we couldn't explain it."

Tests showed a small drop in the weight of objects placed over the device, as if it were shielding the object from the effects of gravity, an effect deemed impossible by most scientists. "We thought it might be a mistake," Dr Podkletnov said, "but we have taken every precaution." Yet the bizarre effects persisted. The team found that even the air pressure vertically above the device dropped slightly, with the effect detectable directly above the device on every floor of the laboratory.

The Finnish team is already expanding its program, to see if it can amplify the anti-gravity effect. In its latest experiments, the team has measured a 2 percent drop in the weight of objects suspended over the device, and double that if one device is suspended over another. If the team can increase the effect substantially, the commercial implications are enormous, that is, if the secret government doesn't try to suppress further research by civilian scientists.

Chapter 9

RUSSIA'S HIDDEN 'DEATH STAR' AND LUNAR BASE

SECRET BLACK PROJECTS OF THE NEW WORLD ORDER

Although the Cold War is apparently over, one reason that the United States may feel compelled to build secret aircraft and exotic weapons is that other countries may have exotic weapon systems of their own. In February 1992, Russian President, Boris Yeltsin, proposed to the United States and the United Nations to develop a global defense shield (with "Star Wars" type weapons) based on Russian Technology.

Some might wonder what the Russian's could have developed in the way of Space Weapon's technology since the United States has claimed that the Soviets couldn't keep up with high technology development. The little-known truth is that the Russians started deploying an operational "Star Wars" defense system in 1977, and it has greatly grown and improved since then. It is a space triad, built around charged-particle beam and neutron particle beam weapons.

In September 1977 the Russians started launching manned killer satellites, called "Cosmo's Interceptors," armed with charged-particle beam weapons, into earth orbit. By April 1978 there were about thirty-six satellites in orbit, by that time they had reportedly destroyed all American spy and early warning satellites.

On September 27, 1977, a Cosmos Interceptor in Earth orbit used a neutron-particle beam weapon to wipe out a secret American laser-beam base nearing operational status in Copernicus Crater on the moon. The Russians then quickly deployed their own military bases on the moon. This was the second leg of their space triad, starting on October 4, 1977, with seven charged-particle beam weapon bases on the near side of the moon, and three support bases on the far side.

The first test of the moon base weapons occurred on November 19, 1977, ironically at about the same time as the release of the first "Star Wars" movie with its "Death Star" weapon. The Russians were aiming at the eye of a cyclone near India. However, they miscalculated the deflection of the beam by the Earth's magnetic field, and the beam struck the ocean too close to the shore causing a tidal wave that killed hundreds of people in Indiaand Bangladesh. A blast of charged-particle beams from two or more of the Russian moon bases fired in quick succession would create the destructive effect of a hydrogen bomb.

The third leg of Russia's triad of space weapons is the "Cosmospheres." The first-generation Cosmospheres were weapon's platforms that were Electrogravtic, powered by nuclear reactors. The ships were horizontally positioned by rocket thrusters, and were invisible to radar beyond about 40 miles, possibly from a stealth-like radar-absorbing coating on their surface.

The Cosmospheres were armed with charged-particle beam weapons and equipped with "Psycho-energetic range finding," which tunes into the actual atomic signature of a target or object and cannot be jammed. Some of these craft were also armed with microwave brain-scrambling equipment.

In late 1977 and early 1978, there was a strange rash of air booms along the east coast of the United States. These air booms were never satisfactorily explained, by either the government, the scientific establishment, or the news media. The mystery explosions couldn't be positively identified with any particular Super Sonic Transport plane (SST) or other aircraft, and indeed they were much louder than aircraft sonic booms.

The giant airbooms were actually caused by Russian Cosmospheres firing charged particle beams down into the atmosphere. The main purpose of any "Star Wars" defense system is to protect a country against nuclear attack. During the weekend of January 20, 1980, Russian Cosmospheres accomplished such a mission.

SECRET BLACK PROJECTS OF THE NEW WORLD ORDER

A nuclear first strike against Russia, by the United States, was ordered with a total of 82 secret, black budget aircraft. These aircraft reportedly could sneak up to a country's shoreline under water, surface, change configuration, take off, and fly at treetop level to their targets. The "subcraft" were sent to the Caspian Sea and off northern Norway.

Late Saturday night, Washington time, a coded signal was flashed to the Subcraft to continue as planned. By that time, the northern contingent of Subcraft were in the White Sea. The southern contingent had reached the north end of the Caspian Sea. It was already daylight, Sunday morning the 20th, for the Subcraft contingents.

Their orders were to wait out the day under water, out of sight. Then after nightfall, they were to continue their steady approach to get close to their targets. The Subcraft were maintaining strict radio silence. They were also deep enough under water to be invisible from the air to either the eye or radar, yet they were hugging the shoreline in water too shallow for Russian sonar to pick them up.

The Russians, using disinformation tactics, deployed their Navy to the Arabian Sea, pretending to be fooled by the United States distraction with their aircraft carriers. In this way, the Russians encouraged the Pentagon to launch the Subcraft toward their targets. However, the black budget subcraft were being tracked by Cosmospheres overhead using "Psycho-energetic range finding."

Shortly after 1:00 AM Sunday morning Eastern Standard Time, the Cosmospheres began firing their charged particle beam weapons. There were ten Subcraft in the White Sea. Each disappeared in a blinding white water spout of steam, smoke, and fire. In the north end of the Caspian there were 19 Subcraft, they, too, met the same fate. Thus averting what could have been a worldwide nuclear holocaust.

SECRET BLACK PROJECTS OF THE NEW WORLD ORDER

The Russian's continue to maintain their exotic weapon's systems. The cost to the Russian's unfortunately has been extremely high. Problems in the Russian economy could be because of the high cost of maintaining their defense system. The 3rd-generation Russian Jumbo Cosmospheres were first deployed in April 1981, in parallel with the first U.S. Space Shuttle mission.

Jumbo Cosmospheres are much larger than the 1st generation models, and use Electromagnetic Propulsion instead of rocket thrusters to move around. In 1984, Russian Jumbo Cosmospheres captured two communication satellites right after launch from U.S. Space Shuttle Mission #10. The Russians found anti-satellite missiles mounted on one satellite and dumped both satellites into useless orbits.

ALTERNATIVE FORM OF ENERGY

By now, you may be curious to know what form this energy takes and where it may be obtained from. You may also wonder why you have not heard of this startling disclosure before now. The answers to such questions are very simple:
- The energy is FREE ENERGY!
- It is available all around you —from the very air itself!
- And the reason you have not been told anything about it is because there is a massive conspiracy afoot on the part of the military–industrial complex to keep its existence a closely-guarded secret from the "masses of asses," who it is felt, should remain in total ignorance so that the "corporate interests" can continue to rake in huge profits at the sake of life and limb—mainly ours!

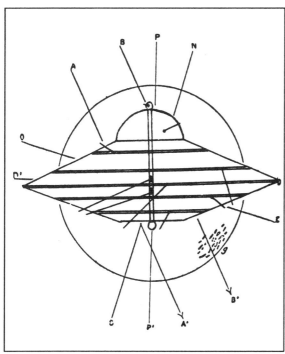

Chapter 10

CIA AND KGB CHATTER... WHO HAS THE EDGE?

SECRET BLACK PROJECTS OF THE NEW WORLD ORDER

Reports have surfaced that the Soviets have had confrontational encounters with UFOs and Extraterrestrials. After Mikhail Gorbachev dissolved in 1991 the KGB top-secret intelligence administration, secret material from that department found its way to the CIA.

As reported by the authoritative magazine, *Canadian Weekly World News*, U.S. intelligence obtained a 250-page file on the attack by a UFO on a military unit in Siberia. The file contains not only many documentary photographs and drawings, but also testimonies by actual participants in the events. One of the CIA representatives referred to this case as "a horrific picture of revenge on the part of extraterrestrial creatures, a picture that makes one's blood freeze."

According to the KGB materials, a low-flying UFO in the shape of a saucer appeared above a military unit that was conducting routine training maneuvers. For unknown reasons, somebody unexpectedly launched a surface-to-air missile and hit the UFO. It fell to earth not far away, and five short humanoids with "large heads and large black eyes" emerged from it.

It was stated in the testimonies by the two soldiers who remained alive that, after freeing themselves from the debris, the aliens came close together and then "merged into a single object that acquired a spherical shape." That object began to buzz and hiss sharply, and then became brilliant white.

In a few seconds, the spheres grew much bigger and exploded by flaring up with an extremely bright light. At that very instant, 23 soldiers who had watched the phenomenon turned into stone poles. Only two soldiers who stood in the shade and were less exposed to the luminous explosion survived.

SECRET BLACK PROJECTS OF THE NEW WORLD ORDER

The KGB report goes on to say that the remains of the UFO and the "petrified soldiers" were transferred to a secret scientific research institution near Moscow. Specialists assume that a source of energy that is still unknown to earthlings instantly changed the structure of the soldiers' living organisms, having transformed it into a substance whose molecular composition is no different from that of limestone. A CIA representative stated, "If the KGB file corresponds to reality, this is an extremely menacing case. The aliens possess such weapons and technology that go beyond all our assumptions. They can stand up for themselves if attacked."

The March 31, 1997 issue of *Defense Weekly* ran the story, "Air Force organizes for offensive info war." According to the article, the US Air Force has created the position of deputy director for information operations. An "Offensive Information Warfare" division will be created under the new deputy director. The division will have the organizational code AF/XOIOW and will be headed by Lt. Col. Jimmy Miyamoto. Offensive information warfare, which implies attacks on both military and civilian targets, is among the least discussed aspect of the Air Force's moves to organize, train and equip the service for information dominance, the article admits.

The new information Operations office will coordinate with the Pentagon's Joint Chiefs of Staff, National Security Agency, Defense Intelligence Agency, Central Intelligence Agency, National Reconnaissance Office, Defense Airborne Reconnaissance Office and the National Imagery and Mapping Agency. New research efforts are under way to support this new program, including: Lethal HPM munitions.

The USAF Office of Scientific Research is working on developing a small affordable laser and high-powered microwave for unmanned aerial vehicles such as the ones possibly being tested at Groom Lake Complexes (Area 51) in Nevada, General Aerodynamics facility by El Mirage Dry Lake, north of McDonnell-Douglas radar cross-section site near Llano, California. These vehicles would be used to perform a variety of missions, including enemy communications

SECRET BLACK PROJECTS OF THE NEW WORLD ORDER

and computer systems monitoring.

SOFTWARE VIRUSES

Software viruses are being developed to be placed or injected into enemy weapons and information links. These viruses would remain dormant until activated by satellite, aircraft radar, or jamming equipment, etc. When activated, the virus would render the equipment useless, or better yet, "there could be a very subtle change for a finite period of time." A country's entire computer network could be completely destroyed by the careful insertion of one or more destructive viruses. Defense against a computer virus is almost hopeless because of the ever growing types of virus being developed. As soon as you come out with an anti virus program, there is a new generation of viruses in which there is no cure.

The article describes a quasi-information warfare/psychological operations program that was first discussed in the Air Force after Desert Storm. Holographic projection involves projection of a three-dimensional holographic image in project decoys, or even an "angry god" (religious imagery) above the battlefield.

The Pentagon had listed the holographic projections openly as part of its "non-lethal" weapons program. However, since 1994, the program has disappeared from view, evidently now a "BLACK" effort, says *Defense Week*. In conclusion, the article states that the Army's JFK Special Warfare Center and School in late 1991 disclosed that it was looking to develop a PSYOPS Hologram System with a capability to "project persuasive messages and three-dimensional pictures of cloud, smoke, raindroplets, buildings. The use of holograms as a persuasive message will have worldwide application."

Chapter ll

EXPOSING THE REALITY OF 'LEVEL SEVEN'

SECRET BLACK PROJECTS OF THE NEW WORLD ORDER

In 1984, President Reagan in a public address deliberately, or inadvertently, let slip the remarks that the world may one day unite to fight a threat from outer space. This was followed by a series of subsequent remarks during the latter days of his term of office. The basic information revealing the existence of Operation Majestic-12, the crashed UFOs, alien beings, and their secret bases within the United States, was obtained through the Freedom of Information Act from the files of the CIA, NSA, FBI, State Department, and the U.S. Air Force.

These documents reveal the "Above Top Secret" nature of Operation Majestic-12. They also verify that the scientific discovery of all time has been hidden from the people of Earth, and that both communications and relationships with extraterrestrial alien beings have already been achieved. The belief that the secret government has built underground bases is widespread within the UFO/conspiracy community. Rumor has it that some of these bases were given over to extraterrestrials by the hidden government.

There is no denying that secret underground bases do exist. In the book, *Underground Bases and Tunnels*, author Richard Sauder reveals that several such facilities have become public knowledge following the fall of the USSR, including Mt.Weather in Virginia. What may be surprising to some is that the facility at Mt. Weather, established as an emergency White House, is under the administration of the Federal Emergency Management Agency (FEMA).

A 1989 article in the *U.S. News and World Report* stated that FEMA and the Pentagon administer some 50 secret underground command posts, including Mt. Weather, and a Pentagon backup facility called "Raven Rock" or "Site R" near the Maryland-Pennsylvania border. This site is relatively near the presidential retreat "Camp David," which is thought to possibly have its own underground complex. Sauder points out that if such a complex exists, it is at least conceivable that the two underground complexes may be linked. However, that is only speculation.

SECRET BLACK PROJECTS OF THE NEW WORLD ORDER

Part of the difficulty one has in trying to unravel this mystery is that it has become linked with national defense. Most of the early underground facilities were apparently connected to our nuclear testing program, with some more complex plans outlining deep storage MX missile silos. Some of those plans include mechanical borers that would tunnel to the surface through the rubble of a nuclear attack, pulling a MX missile behind them. Once the borers reach the surface they move out of the way and the missiles they have in tow could be fired in retaliation.

These are doomsday scenarios that are the stuff of science fiction, and appear to only scratch the surface of what has been proposed over the past four decades. Sauder reveals that the U.S. Intelligence community became aware of a tunnel system beneath Moscow that leaders of that country could use to survive a nuclear attack. This became known in the early 1960s, and it could reasonably be speculated that efforts soon got underway to construct such facilities for the leadership of the United States.

However, to be effective these facilities had to be completely secret. To accomplish this, technologies had to be developed to construct such underground facilities, and methodologies had to be developed that would allow their construction to remain unnoticed by those who live nearby.

To understand the significance of what can be done, one only has to look as far as the Greebrier Hotel, in White Sulphur Springs, WV. When the story broke in 1992, only six Members of Congress were aware of the construction of living quarters, meeting rooms, banks of computers, and communications equipment installed in an underground complex at the Hotel. The entrance to this facility was protected by two 20 ton blast doors, and had been designed to house Members of Congress in the event of an attack. One can only speculate how Members would be notified of the need to travel to the mountains of West Virginia in case of an emergency.

SECRET BLACK PROJECTS OF THE NEW WORLD ORDER

Not only do these facilities exist, but also, they are able to exist beneath a community without its knowledge. As outlined by Sauder, technologies have been suggested that seem more like "Buck Rogers" than current capabilities would seem to allow for. A 1974 Bechtel report included such proposed boring techniques as "Plasma," "Microwaves," "Electron Beam Gun," and "Electrical Disintegration."
This is not idle speculation from a think tank. Sauder's research showed patents had been issued to the US Atomic Energy Commission and the US Energy Research and Development Administration for Subterrene technology.

There is no record of its construction, but the borer (vehicle) would use a liquid metal cooled atomic reactor to generate enough heat to melt its way through rock, just as a worm moves through soil, leaving a glass surfaced tunnel in its wake. Again, this sounds like science fiction, but it appears that some of this technology is already patented. It should be noted that the U.S. Patent office issues patents on viable technology, and not on what "might" be possible.

This, of course, leads to further speculation about vast tunnels that have been created, linking unknown underground bases. If the secret underground bases have been built, such tunnels are certainly possible, but Sauder admits that they would be part of a "black budget" technology and details aren't available.

One proposed defense plan called for the creation of several hundred miles of tunnels in the western states. However, there is no record of those plans being carried out. Some projects outlined on paper would create facilities more than a mile and a half below the surface, but again there is no information detailing if these projects were actually completed.

Glowing globes of hovering and darting lights have made their home in the skies above both America as well as countries around the world without official acknowledgement of the existence of what have become known as UFOs.

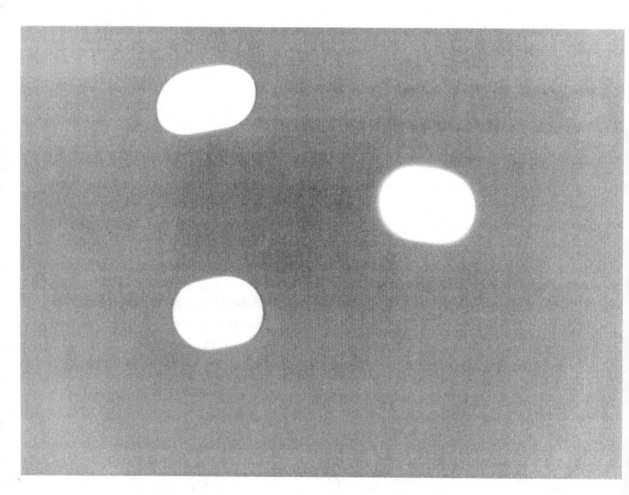

SECRET BLACK PROJECTS OF THE NEW WORLD ORDER

While one would expect to find the Defense and Intelligence agencies involved in the construction of underground facilities, the involvement of FEMA, the National Science Foundation (NSA), the Federal Highway Administration (FHA), the Urban Mass Transit Authority (UMTA), and others was somewhat of a surprise. Indeed, some facilities known to exist are owned by defense contractors, and not the federal government, which adds another layer of complexity to this mix.

Sauder considers that this technology has been around for so long, that some of the facilities are becoming completely outdated. One such facility in New England was actually listed with a local real estate firm for sale. The price of this used underground facility was $250,000, and, given its original cost, that was probably a steal.

One of the more interesting points made relates to what could be, rather than what is proven. Sauder has uncovered documents from the 1980s prepared by Los Alamos Laboratories and Texas A&M University (under a NASA contract) that discuss the use of "nuclear tunneling machines" to melt tunnels beneath the surface of the moon. This would be done to create an environment for human occupation in a lunar colony.

The cost of such a project was estimated at about $50 million to create the tunneling machine, and between $155 million and $2.3 billion dollars to transport it to the moon's surface. While these figures seem high, they represent only a fraction of the black budget, which would be used to fund such a project outside of public scrutiny.

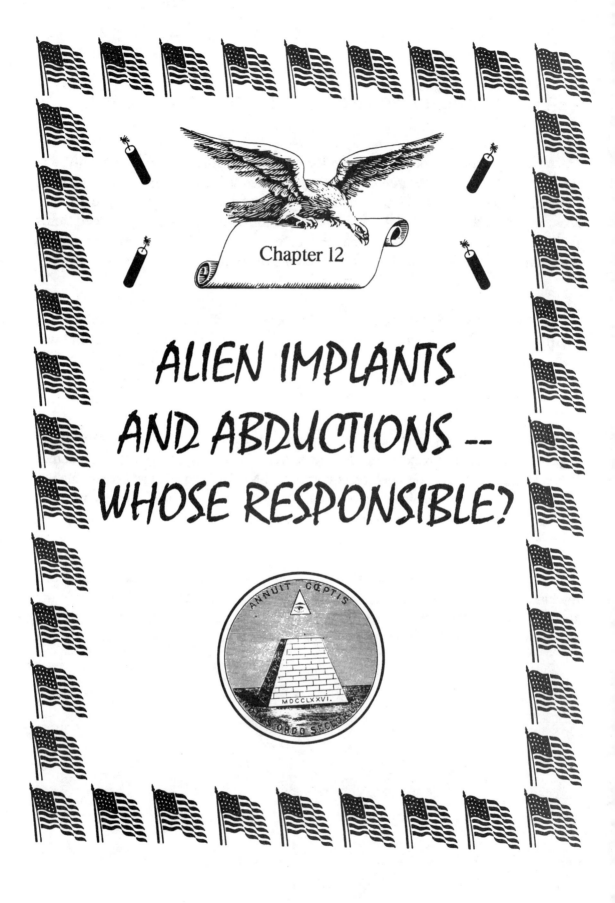

Chapter 12

ALIEN IMPLANTS AND ABDUCTIONS -- WHOSE RESPONSIBLE?

ANNUIT COEPTIS

MDCCLXXVI.

ORDO SECLORUM

SECRET BLACK PROJECTS OF THE NEW WORLD ORDER

The recent phenomenon of alleged UFO abductions has brought forth some evidence that extraterrestrials are not responsible for all of the kidnappings. In an article entitled: *Evidence for military kidnappings of alleged UFO-abductees*, author Dr. Helmut Lammer Ph.D. cites information that the abductees were in fact taken by humans to secret underground bases. Several abductees have recalled seeing military/intelligence personnel in these secret facilities.

Most abductees report the involvement of military/intelligence personnel after seeing black helicopters flying above their homes. Debby Jordan reports, for instance, in a side note of her book *Abducted!*, that she was stunned from an alleged friend and brought to a kind of underground hospital where she was examined by a medical doctor, who removed an implant from her ear.

The abduction experiences of Leah Haley and Katharina Wilson are full of military/underground base encounters. Some of Katharina Wilson's experiences are comparable with mind control experiments. She experienced a flashback from her childhood where she remembers being in a hospital where she was forced into a Skinner Box-like container that was possibly used for behavior modification experiments.

Experiencers describe activity of black helicopters, the appearance of strange vans or buses outside the houses of abductees, exposure to disorienting electromagnetic fields, drugging, transport with a helicopter, bus or truck to an unknown building or an underground military facility. Usually there are physical aftereffects, like grogginess and sometimes nausea after the kidnaping. There is also a difference when the abductors appear. In most UFO-abduction cases, the beings appear through a closed window, wall, or the abductee feels a strange presence in the room.

SECRET BLACK PROJECTS OF THE NEW WORLD ORDER

Most abductees report that they are paralyzed from the mental power of the alien beings. With the secret military abductions, the abductee reports that the kidnappers give him or her a shot with a syringe. It is interesting, that secret military abductees report that they are examined by human doctors in rectangular rooms and not in round sterile rooms, as in descriptions of UFO-abductees. The described rooms, halls and furniture are similar to terrestrial hospital rooms, laboratories or research facilities and have nothing to do with UFOs.

We must consider the possibility that some information we are getting from military abductees may be cover stories, induced by hypnoprogramming processes of military psychiatrists. There is also the possibility that the military personnel use rubber alien masks and special effects during an abduction. Katharina Wilson reports flashbacks where she thinks that she held a rubber mask of an alien in their hands.

These facts lead some mind control researchers to believe that all alien abductees are used in secret mind control and/or genetic experiments, staged by a powerful black arm of the US government. However, some questions do remain:

■ If all UFO-abductions are indeed a cover for secret mind control or genetic experiments like the Lebensborn-Project of the Nazis, why do abductees report military/intelligence involvement since the early eighties and not before? We should see the opposite in this pattern, since the mind control technology should be much better in the nineties than during the sixties and seventies.

■ Why are there mind control victims who are implanted and used for secret weapon tests, but have nothing to do with the UFO phenomenon or alien abductions? It seems that the mind control agenda wouldn't need UFO-abductions as a cover story, since nobody believes the claims of ordinary mind control victims, although they have x-rays where everyone can see anomalous objects in their heads.

SECRET BLACK PROJECTS OF THE NEW WORLD ORDER

■   If all UFO-abductions are a cover for mind control experiments, why is the military interested in gynecological examinations of female abductees?

Of course serious researchers should investigate all possibilities, some UFO-abductees may be mind control victims or used in black project genetic experiments. However, there exists another possibility for a motive that is more plausible for the military involvement in the UFO-abduction phenomenon, since it describes the military abduction pattern better. Secret military abductions may be the evidence that a secret military/intelligence task force has operated since the early eighties in North America and is involved in monitoring and kidnaping of alleged UFO-abductees.

In the beginning of the eighties a lot of money became available for top-secret military projects like the Strategic Defense Initiative (SDI). This task force might be financed by a portion of this money. It seems that they are interested in well investigated UFO-abduction cases. They are monitoring the houses of their victims, kidnaping and possible implanting them with military devices sometimes shortly after an UFO-abduction experience. Implants were being used on unwitting persons as early as fifty years ago.

One well-documented case of the implantation of an electronic device into a victim is the case of Robert Naeslund. Mr. Naeslund claims that he was unwittingly implanted during an operation in Stockholm, Sweden. He has x-rays that show clearly a mushroom-shaped device in his brain. He claims that the operation was performed by Dr. Curt Strand, who inserted the device in his head through the right nasal passage. Interestingly, UFO-abductees report since the sixties how alien beings implanted them by placing small objects up their nose through the nasal passage and sinus cavity.

SECRET BLACK PROJECTS OF THE NEW WORLD ORDER

It appears that the military could be searching for possible alien implants. Their gynecological interest on female abductees could be explained, if they are searching for alleged alien/hybrid embryos, since most of the abducted females had missing embryo/fetus experiences. However, one thing is for sure, this task force or the people who are behind these kidnapings using advanced mind control technology that is currently tested illegally on people who might have nothing to do with UFO abductions.

Chapter 13

TARGET EARTH: WHEN WILL THE SECRET GOVERNMENT STRIKE NEXT?

SECRET BLACK PROJECTS OF THE NEW WORLD ORDER

On Sunday morning April 2, 1978, a mysterious explosion rocked the Canadian community of Lance Cove, Bell Island, Newfoundland. Streaks of silvery-white light shot out of the sky, shaking homes for miles around. The town's electrical system was shorted out, and many homes experienced power surges that caused televisions to explode and electrical outlets to be blown off the walls. This unusual blast was detected by satellite, registering as a "potential nuclear blast."

Reports of mysterious booms and "air explosions" were recorded all along the eastern seaboard of the United States and Canada during 1977 and 1978. The strange explosion over Bell Island had been preceded by sightings of unusual lights over nearby Conception Bay on Saturday night. One observer, who phoned his report to radio station VOCM, said that the UFOs were orange, green and white lights that moved erraticly across the sky.

A woman from Portugal Cove, two-and-a-half miles from Bell Island, reported that she saw a straight beam of white light coming down from the sky at a 45 degree angle. The light had a strange gleam to it, and there was a rumble from the ground when the beam struck. Shortly thereafter, Bell Island was hit by a powerful explosion. Could this incident have been caused by a high powered microwave beam? Possibly test shot from an orbiting satellite? The Bell Island incident indicates that the area was indeed struck by a high-energy source of some kind. After the blast, tests for high radiation determined that the explosion was not caused by a nuclear device. However, an electromagnetic pulse accompanying the blast could explain the damage suffered to electical lines and in-house wiring all across the area.

The unusual blast did extensive damage on the property of James Bickford. According to Bickford, around 11AM he was startled by a huge flash of white light, accompanied by a thunderous explosion. Seconds before, Mrs. Bickford had heard what she described as hailstones hitting her window in the bedroom. She left the room and was passing the fuse box in the hall, when she felt a terrible pressure in her head. She put her hands up to her ears just as the blast hit the area. The nearby fuse box exploded as electricity (possibly caused by a electromagnetic pulse) surged through the power lines. The power surge also blew the light switches from the wall, as well as completely shattering the screen of the TV set. The power surge was so intense that fuses were blown completely out of their sockets and across the room.

In addition to the damage in the main house, the Bickford's nearby summer cabin also received unusual damage. The cabin's roof had been split open and parts of the ceiling had caved in. Inside, a small cupboard where electric wires entered the building had been shattered by the powerful surge of electricity. There were also indications that power had surged through the metal water pipes and other metal objects in the cabin.

The top of a nearby barn and chicken coop were almost completely ripped off by the explosion, and dead chickens were found in the ruins of the coop. The chickens appeared to have been killed not only from the concussion of the blast, but also from strong electric shocks from the possible electromagnetic pulse.

After the blast, two holes were discovered behind the barn. The largest was almost two feet deep. The dirt from the holes appeared to have been gouged out of the ground and flung some distance away. One hole was found under a fir tree that had suffered extensive burning about a quarter of its height of twenty feet. There was no evidence in or around the holes to indicate that they could have been produced by meteorites.

Many eye-witnesses to the strange incident reported that a bright flash of light was seen right before the explosion. A cousin of the Bickfords who lives nearby desribed what she saw. "I was standing at the counter in my kitchen, peeling potatoes into an old metal tray when the explosion occurred. My back was to the

SECRET BLACK PROJECTS OF THE NEW WORLD ORDER

It has long been a theme of artists as to who might be in control of humankind...be it "The Controllers" Commander X speaks of, or perhaps the dreaded secret societies to be found in occult literature.

window when suddenly flames rose up to my face from the tray, everything around me shook, and I thought that heaven and earth had come togeather. My son's girlfriend ran in and said that she saw the meadow towards Mr. Bickford's place light up like a great flame."

Carol O'Brien, a neighbor who lives down the road from the Bickford property, said that she had at first heard "a rumbling sound which seemed to come closer. Then the room I was in lit up with a bright light. I could see the sky was a bright red, and there was smoke. I first thought that a house down the road had exploded, but when the smoke cleared I could see the house was still intact. My little brother who was lying on the floor, saw a shot of light come out from the oven door, right through the glass. He said it looked like a lighting bolt or a ray gun blast you see on television."

Shortly afterwards, Lance Cove was visited by several scientists who had heard about the mysterious event. Dr. Ken Collerson, a Memorial University meteorologist, said he was interested in the visual sightings and the unusual sounds. Dr. Tom Gold from Cornell University in Ithasa, NY, arrived to investigate the occurrence terming it a "most unusual and interesting phenomenon." The *St. John's Evening Telegraph* reported that soon after the incident, two military attaches from a U.S. defense center visited Bell Island "taking care not to attract the attention of the news media." It was never known what caused the strange explosion, or what the military attaches were looking for.

According to *Aviation & Space Technology* (April 10, 1995), the USAF has recently acquired a 15-million-watt generator from the former Soviet Union that can blast targets with deadly accuracy from hidden sites, or from aircraft, and even outer space. The generator is designed to power a steady-state weapon like a laser for six to ten seconds. An Air Force researcher states, "Or, with some sort of power conversion, it could be used to fire a high-powered microwave weapon."

SECRET BLACK PROJECTS OF THE NEW WORLD ORDER

The secret black budget military has been experimenting with electromagnetic weapon systems for many years. Evidence suggests that such weapons may have been developed in the closing days of World War II. In his book *Inside the Third Reich*, Albert Speer quoted Dr. Robert Ley, head of the Nazi Labor Front, as saying he had designed a "death ray" which would prove to be the "decisive weapon" against American and Russian troops closing in on Berlin in April, 1945. It is possible that at the end of the war that Dr. Ley's papers fell into the hands of the Americans who continued research up into the present.

The March 1988 issue of *Spectrum*, the official publication of the Institute of Electrical and Electronics Engineers, confirms that Sandia National Laboratories has been active in the field of electromagnetic-pulse weaponry. According to the publication, a special research team led by Eugene C. Cnare successfully tested a miniaturized plasma-generating device, capable of being applied to high powered microwave missiles and gravity bombs.

The black budget, secret weapon conspiracy continues. It may never be known just what kinds of exotic aircraft, death ray weapons, and giant leaps in science have been accomplished. Nor will it likely be soon revealed whether these exotic weapons and aircraft were constructed purely by ourselves, or with the help of extraterrestrials. What is known, is that unless the citizens of the world band together and demand that the secret governments come clean about their hidden programs of destruction, the possibility is very real that the innocent people of planet Earth will become the unwitting victims of the same science and technology that was conceived to protect and preserve their way of life.

A FEW FACTS
ABOUT AUTHOR
TIM SWARTZ

Emmy Award
Winning Producer

Tim Swartz is an Emmy-Award winning television producer who for more than twenty years has been actively involved with research and investigation of UFOs and paranormal phenomenon.

A world traveler, Swartz has visited many of the world's most sacred sites such as Stonehenge, the pyramids of Egypt, and the great wall of China.

In his career as a television videographer/producer, the author has met and conferred with world leaders as well as noted experts in the field of Mystic Sciences and UFOlogy.

Tim is also an expert in various forms of divination, dowsing, spiritual communications and metaphysics in general.

Lately, he has spearheaded an investigation into mind control as well as other government and military related conspiracies that have become popularized on the Internet and in the mass media.

Two Uncomfortable titles from Alex Constantine

PSYCHIC DICTATORSHIP IN THE U.S.A.

■ WARNING: This book is sure to shatter the reader's delusions about its own government for "bombing minds rather than bodies is the warfare of the new millennium," says the author who uncovers the terrifying extent of electromagnetic and biotelemetric mind control experimentation in involuntary human subjects. This volume tracks the use of cults by intelligence organizations as "cover" for: √ Arms sales; √ Mind control, and even √ Child abuse to create assassins with multiple personality syndrome. √ The Army's body-bag connection and a triple murder in N.C. √ Plus a chapter titled, "Funny Money -Johnny Carson, the CIA and S&L Crisis."
 Over 200 pages of documented "monkey business." $15.00. Order by title or Code: BPD.

VIRTUAL GOVERNMENT: CIA MIND CONTROL OPERATIONS IN AMERICA

■ Includes vital information on: x Drug and mob connections in the Simpson murder case. x Integration of Nazis into American intelligence. x CIA experiments on children. x Mind control within the Postal Service. x Infestation of media by CIA operatives. x Rise of Timothy McVeigh from robot to bomber. GUARANTEED you won't put this "real life" thriller down! Order by title or Code: BVG, $15.00.

Order From:
GLOBAL COMMUNICATIONS
P. O. Box 753, New Brunswick, NJ 08903
Credit Card Orders --
(732) 602-3407
Add $4.00 for Priority Shipping

ADDITIONAL BEST SELLERS BY "COMMANDER X"

A FORMER MILITARY INTELLIGENCE OPERATIVE SPEAKS OUT!

COSMIC PATRIOT FILES

2 VOLUME SET

From the "Committee of 12 to Save the Earth"

Hundreds of topics are covered in this closely typeset, two volume—shrink-wrapped—set that has been specifically compiled for the student of New Age conspiracies.

Included are such intriguing, mind-boggling subjects as: • Founding of the Secret Order of the Illuminati. • Mystical significance of the layout of Washington, D.C., and the placement of the Washington Monument, the Pentagon and actual streets and other geographical locations. • Identification of global leaders involved in a conspiracy to formulate a "New World Order"—or "One World Government," and why they would want to do so. • Use of unmarked helicopters in keeping an eye on dissident citizens (including UFO witnesses) • Hitler's use of negative Occult influence and how these influences are still alive even today! • The responsibility for controlling the economy of the world. • The Great AIDS Cover-up revealed. • Activities of the "Brotherhood of Shadows" exposed. • Why Kennedy was shot.
ISBN: 0-938294-06-7 8-1/2x11—two volumes **$39.95**

THE ULTIMATE DECEPTION

This is a conspiracy that leads right up to the front gate of the White House, and involves the agreement forged between the military and a group of ETs referred to as the EBEs (short for Extraterrestrial Biological Entities). As part of this conspiracy, the government has literally "sold out" our citizens by extending to the EBEs the right to abduct humans and to plant monitoring devices in their brains, in exchange for technical and scientific data. "Our only hope for survival," says Commander X, "is a second group of benevolent ETs—most commonly referred to as the 'Nordic-types' —who believe in the universal law of 'non-interference.'"
ISBN: 0-938294-99-7 6x9 **$15.00**

UNDERGROUND ALIEN BASES

Aliens have established bases around the planet. An ancient tunnel system has existed on Earth since the time of Atlantis. Entrance ways can be found in many major cities. Some government and military officials have taken the side of the aliens. Here are bizarre stories about underground bases at Dulce, New Mexico; Groom Lake, Nevada; South and North Pole; Mt. Shasta, California, as well as in the Andes. Here also are the first-hand reports of individuals who have been abducted, and have survived genetic experiments in these locations.
ISBN: 0-938294-92-X 6x9 **$15.00**

NIKOLA TESLA—FREE ENERGY AND THE WHITE DOVE

Here are Top Secret revelations concerning a newly-developed antigravity aircraft currently being tested inside Nevada's remote *Area 51*, as disclosed by a former military intelligence operative. This aircraft, which can fly three times higher and faster than any officially recognized plane or rocket, is based upon an invention of Nikola Tesla, one of the greatest "free thinkers" of all times, who arrived upon our cosmic shores in order to shape our technical and spiritual destiny. Tesla, the author reveals, came from another place to alert the world of impending danger (World Wars I and II), while at the same time offering "helpful solutions" to our problems and alternatives by which to greatly enhance our lives.

In addition to previously unpublished material on Tesla's Other-Worldly "roots," here also are full details of the ongoing work of such modern-day inventors as Otis T. Carr, Arthur H. Matthews and Howard Menger, who have perfected alternative methods of propulsion.
ISBN: 0-938294-82-2 6x9 **$15.00**

THE CONTROLLERS

We are the property of an alien Intelligence! "Our" planet is a cosmic laboratory and we are but guinea pigs to those who have kept us prisoners on Earth. Humankind continues to face an all-out battle with those who have kept us as their slaves for centuries. Down through history, they have been known by different names: The Soulless Ones, The Elders, The Dero, The Grays, The Illuminati and The Counterfeit Race. Yet, very few know the real identity and purpose of *The Controllers*, a strange, parallel race that is metaphysically programmed to do evil and, according to authorities, has complete control of our education process, major philanthropic foundations, the banking system, the media, as well as dominant influence over all worldly governments.
ISBN: 0-938294-42-3 8-1/2x11—shrink-wrapped **$19.95**

THE PHILADELPHIA EXPERIMENT CHRONICLES—EXPLORING THE STRANGE CASE OF ALFRED BIELEK & DR. M.K. JESSUP

For the first time, a survivor tells his remarkable story of a career of brainwashing by the military, and how he eventually came to unlock the mysterious facts about what happened decades ago. Also reveals the case of famed scientist Dr. Morris K. Jessup, who died under mysterious circumstances because he knew too much about the Philadelphia Experiment. ISBN: 0-938294-00-8 **$15.00**

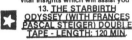

WHAT IS TO COME DURING THE NEXT MILLENNIUM???